~~GENDER~~
ISSUES
-
IN AFRICAN LITERATURE

Smith and Ce [ed.]

AFRICAN
Library of Critical Writing

GENDER ISSUES - in African Literature
©Smith and Ce (Ed.)

©African Library of Critical Writing
Print Edition
ISBN:978-9-7837-0854-9

For information address:
Progeny (Press) International
Email: progeny.int@gmail.com
For: African Books Network
9 Handel Str.
AI EBS Nigeria WA
Email: handelbook@gmail.com

Marketing and Distribution in the US, UK,
Europe, N. America (Canada),
and Commonwealth countries by

African Books Collective Ltd.
PO Box 721
Oxford OX1 9EN
United Kingdom
Email: orders@africanbookscollective.com

Contents

Introduction

Chapter 1

Resisting Normative Definitions   *13*

Issues

Chapter 2

Gender Conflict in African Literature   *30*

Chapter 3

Gender and African Modernity   *43*

Chapter 4

Female Writers on War   *65*

Chapter 5

Male Authority, Female Alterity   *90*

Chapter 6

Feminist (Re-) Writing   *110*

Chapter 7

Twice-Betrayed People   *137*

Chat

Chapter 8

Seven Nigerian Authors   *167*

Notes and Bibliography

Introduction

GENDER ISSUES takes a starting note with "Resisting Normative Definitions" which examines the ways in which the protagonist counters and challenges intertwined Western discourses on gender, employment, sexuality, and health in Bessora's novel, *Deux bébés et l'addition*. It interprets mainstream definitions of gender and sexuality as "reliant on specific categorizations based on Cartesian 'taxonomies'" that were prominent in nineteenth century studies of gender and sexuality. This chapter explores the ways in which the central character of Bessora's novel subverts all expectations for masculinity and health placed on him by contemporary French society, thus undermining "notions of sexuality" firmly rooted in the biomedical field and inextricably linked to discussions of health and the "normal" functioning of both body and mind.

Our second Section on Gender has six chapters on African gender conflict in literature with the study of Aminata Fall in "Gender and African Modernity." Here we chronicle contrastive attempts made by two female writers in Africa at countering traditional stereotypical representation of women in their works. While Fall does not clearly portray women in their positive light, her attempt to "counter previous misrepresentations of women in *The Beggars' Strike* is, writ large, a re-emphasis of the female stereotype giving "voice to the various opinions and oppressions men perpetuate in society" while a relatively new Osammor appears to put forward a more positive picture of modern African womanhood.

In Nadine Gordimer's novel, *None to Accompany Me*, Yvonne Vera's, *The Stone Virgins* and Buchi Emecheta's *Destination Biafra*, it has been noted how the extent to which "their common experiences of that reality bring African women writers from different ideological and social camps closer together." Also the conflict between Tradition and Modernity with a study of the Gender Crisis in Chinua Achebe's *No Longer at Ease* and *Anthills of the Savannah*, is argued from bell hooks's favourite premise that while "male supremacist ideology" encourages women to believe they are "valueless and obtain value only by relating to or bonding with men," women however must "unlearn" these false concepts if they are to build "a sustained feminist movement" and "(re)learn the true meaning and value of sisterhood."

There is a bold attempt to reread Achebe as consistent in not only exposing modern colonial lifestyles that offer "only a veneer of older cultural values" but also in arguing along with women that "in order to fight the seemingly oppressive structures that have traditionally discriminated against them, they must disregard their diversity and embrace their unity." For example, the representation of womanhood in Akachi Ezeigbo's *Children of the Eagle* is enough indication that women have since "appropriated the rites of public space to tell and retell their stories to privilege their perspectives, rehabilitate their dilapidated image and affirm their humanity."

The Chapter "Feminist (Re-) Writing," disagrees with an attempt to "equate literary theory and literature with political activism" by blaming "the lack and the lagging behind of feminist criticism in Nigeria and Africa on the absence of women's political movements." It rather asserts that "feminism or the feminist approach to literature calls for more than a verbal assertion or pointing to feminist aesthetics and politics" and that the critic should "identify, .(re)evaluate and ... focus on women and women issues in each work" as well as clarify "whether there is a particularly feminine way of looking at, perceiving, and responding to issues."

In "The Narratives of a Twice-Betrayed People," Vera's last novel, *The Stone Virgins*, is exemplified as a "counter-narrative" to the earlier "pro-nationalist" novel *Nehanda*. The use of the trauma theory and "the concept of witness or testimonio literature" to explore the paradigm of double traumatization of the major character of Vera's novel and its impact for Zimbabwean civil society is an innovative perspective to the writings of the late Zimbabwean writer who died so young and tragically and left a vacuum in contemporary Zimbabwean writing.

The final part of the book features our Chat Forum with seven writers and critics from Nigeria on a debate about the function of literature in conflict Resolution, a theme for an Authors' Colloquium, where the crop of Nigerian writers seem in accord with the notion that literature must function in line with social, economic and political aspirations of society. It is perhaps significant -

for Africa and the World- that African writer(s) must deepen not just their vision (values) but also their craft (language) in order to create literatures that can not only resolve individual and societal conflicts but also endure in the hearts and minds of readers across many generations.

CS and CC

Chapter 1

Resisting Normative Definitions

J.W.Bouchard

Bessora: Resisting Normative Definitions

As race, feminist and gender theories continue to move from general to more localized views of identitarian issues, we bear witness to literary voices who present non-essentialized protagonists emerging from a specific set of cultural and individual factors. French immigrant authors such as Bessora participate in a chorus of "queer" or "abnormal" voices that Spanish theorist Beatriz Preciado calls "les multitudes." Preciado's discussion of "les multitudes" focuses primarily on physical "difference" and the discourses surrounding intersex or transsexual subjectivities within the Western European context. However, her theory could also be applied to figures who retain an "intersex" identity by resisting normative masculine codes of behavior. In both cases, the "abnormal one" disturbs the foundational French ideals of fixed gender identity that have been perpetuated through centuries of universalist discourse. Within this framework, the cultural significance of Yéno, the protagonist and narrator of Bessora's *Deux bébés et l'addition* can be analyzed.

Yéno is indeed transgressive, in that he both counters and challenges Western discourses on gender, employment, sexuality, and health. In *Deux bébés et l'addition*, mainstream definitions of race, gender and sexuality are represented as reliant on specific categorizations, or Cartesian "taxonomies," that revealed themselves most prominently in seventeenth century French colonial projects and nineteenth century studies of gender and sexuality.

A highly political author, all five of Bessora's novels seek to subvert French definitions of race, gender, and sexuality in the immigrant context. An immigrant herself (of Gabonese and Swiss descent), Bessora's literary projects fuse autobiographical content and fictionalized representations of current political realities facing France's immigrant populations. Within this framework, Bessora offers the reader protagonists who simultaneously serve as models of "abnormality" or "difference," and surpass the limiting identitarian categories imposed upon them. Along with racial "difference," Bessora is particularly concerned with issues surrounding gender identity. In a 2002 article on gender, Bessora writes: "Le biologique n'implique pas un rôle social...il n'y existe pas de fait masculine ou feminine, mais des représentations qui se négocient sans cesse." ("La question du genre" 1). To underscore this notion, Bessora gives us protagonists such as Yéno, who goes against all "rôle sociaux" assigned to his gender and is constantly negotiating his unique identity amidst scathing social discourses regarding normative constructions of gender, sexuality, and acceptable forms of employment in the French nation. His identity is particularly problematic in the eyes of the nation because of his ambiguous sexuality and feminized persona.

In France, mainstream conceptions of gender and sexuality are still informed by specific categorizations that revealed themselves most prominently in nineteenth century Western studies of sexology. Firmly rooted in the biomedical field, studies such as those produced by the research of Havelock Ellis and Richard Freiherr Krafft-Ebing were inextricably linked to discussions of health and the "normal body," While both scholars relied on the binary categories of normalcy and inversion, the nuances of their arguments differed greatly. An important difference between Krafft-Ebing and Ellis is they way in which each categorized "inversion" or homosexuality and other "abnormal" sexual behaviors as pathogolical (Krafft-Ebing) or as suppressed desires that are part of normal human sexuality (Ellis). Krafft-Ebing defined these behaviors as paresthesia or "perversion of the sexual instinct" due to misplaced desire onto objects, body parts other than the primary sexual organs, or members of the same sex. However, Ellis's work is well known for its sympathy toward individuals who were attracted to members of the same sex, a certain body part, or an inanimate fetish object, all qualities that apply to Yéno and will be discussed in subsequent portions of this study. He was a pioneering advocate for the right of "inverts" of both sexes to experience erotic pleasure and social acceptance. Whereas Ellis sought to demystify

15

these "normal" behaviors, Krafft-Ebing asserted that these "deviant" sexual practices (such as homosexuality and "cross-dressing") were curable.

Particularly relevant to the French context is this notion that the "sexually deviant" category of homosexuality was viewed as "degenerative," or a regression to a "primitive state." Such selective terminology hacks back to seventeenth-century discourses on the colonized "Other," who was, in the eyes of the French, a savage in need of both spiritual redemption and cultural education. Given France's problematic colonial history, this notion takes on a noteworthy significance in twentieth and twentieth-century discussions of immigration. The homosexual (or "sexually deviant") immigrant is not only doubly "othered" as a result of both race and sexuality, but he is also viewed as a "degenerate" and transgressive element that endangers the health of the French republican nation. In *The Frail Social Body*, Carolyn Dean reveals the importance of "bodily integrity" to the definition of French citizenship. As her study reveals, in interwar France, homosexuality was thought of as so powerful that it could infect or even undo the French "social body." Referring to present day French politics, Preciado expands on this notion of infection or infiltration in a spatial framework:

Le corps de la multitude queer apparaît au centre de ce que j'appellerai, pour reprendre une expression de Deleuze et Guattari, un travail de "déterritorialisation" de l'hétéroseuxalité. Une déterritorialisation qui affecte aussi bien l'espace urbain (il faut donc parler de déterritorialisation de l'espace majoritaire et non de ghetto) que l'espace corporel. (20)

To combat this spatial or "corporal" infiltration of the "Other," France has turned to universalizing discourses, which have historically served as a sort of vaccination for the national body. Thus, French universalism is premised on idea that anyone can become French, so long as they are willing to subscribe to the specific philosophies and ideologies that make up the French nation. Since this time, universalism has been taken to be the defining trait of the French Republic and its most enduring value. It also shapes current political realities and policies on immigration. Until an immigrant is assimilated into the French universal definition of citizenship, he or she is the ultimate "Other." In an article tracing the evolution of French universalist thought, Naomi Schorr writes: "Achieving French identity requires as the wages of assimilation the renunciation of public cultural particularism in the name of France's vaunted particularity, its "singularity," in short, its universalism." (50). As far as identity is concerned, the universal or "default" French identity is, of course, heterosexual and White. As Beatriz Preciado rightly indicates, in France and elsewhere, heterosexuality is not simply the norm, but also an imposed political regime in the Foucauldian sense.

En travaillant dans une perspective déjà explorée par Audre Lorde, Ti-Grace Atkinson, et le manifeste "The Woman - Identified - Woman" des "Radicalesbians", Wittig en était arrivee à décrire l'hétérosexualité non pas comme une pratique sexuelle mais comme un régime politique, comme faisant partie de l'administration des corps et de la gestion calculée de la vie, et relevant de la "biopolitique". Une lecture croisée de Wittig et de Foucault aurait permis dès le début des années 80 de donner une definition de l'hétérosexualité comme technologie bio-politique destinée à produire des corps straight. ("Multitudes queer" 18)

The identitarian requirements imposed by French Universalism have historically supported the form of heterosexual politics described by Preciado. Furthermore, such requirements are racially exclusive. As a result of these stringent, "universal" guidelines (which, in their most extreme form require a denial of the self and all previous cultural affiliations), miscegenation, hybridity and multiculturalism (all contained in the French term métissage) have been at the center of many debates and continue to raise questions on the social, political, cultural, artistic and literary scenes. Many postmodern scholars agree on the erroneous nature of the term miscegenation, (based on the axiom presupposing the existence of different races within the human species that was born out of modern taxonomical practice), however one must to recognize miscegenation as a concrete cultural and social phenomenon as well as a very real way to define a category of individuals according today's French society.

Though Bessora's Yéno is forced into this limited (and limiting) category by French society, he resists such categorizations thanks to his corporal, historical, and psychological individualities and his racial and cultural métissage. In *Deux bébés et l'addition*, Yéno not only transgresses these universal codes, but also undoes them, exemplifying the need for the French nation to recognize its changing population and the need to reorganize the fixed structures that determine "normalcy" and "alterity" within this context.

An entire study could be done on Yéno's racial and cultural métissage as a signifier of difference. Though we might not be able to cover in detail the identitarian and transgressive themes associated with hybridity and race within this particular project, suffice it to say that Yéno's particular form of gender/sexual transgression is intensely heightened by the fact he is the son of a Black, African mother and a White, French father (conceived in a former French colony). In addition to his race, Yéno's performance of his masculinity/femininity - through his choice of career, his ambivalent sexuality, and his troubled relationship with his mother (that results in both physical and psychological illness) – are both transgressive and productive in the French context.

Yéno is the postmodern hero par excellence, and defies all definitions of "normalcy" imposed on him by French republican values. His identity is fragmented, unresolved, and ambiguous. He does not act, and rather allows himself to be acted upon by his sister, Waura, her husband, Modeste, and his love interest, Nidale. In the sections to follow, we will detail the ways in which Yéno transgresses normative definitions of gender, sexuality, and health before moving into a discussion of the productive possibilities associated with the identitarian model he represents.

Performing Gender: The sage-femme

If "gender is an act which has been rehearsed, much as a script survives the particular actors who make use of it, but which requires individual actors in order to be actualized and reproduced as reality once again," (Butler 526) then Yéno is so far off the script that no social "prompt" of gender normalcy could hope to remind him of the "correct" line. Yéno works as a sage-femme (midwife) in the novel. In French, as in English, there is no specifically masculine term for a "male midwife." This semantic restriction, indicative of the highly gendered nature of the profession, prohibits Yéno from being truly "masculine" in the eyes of the French. Throughout the novel, Yéno is asked by both French and immigrant mothers who come into the hospital why he didn't become a gynecologist, which would have been a more acceptable form of employment for a man. He is considered to be a professional failure, opting for an inferior, feminine position. The reason for Yéno's professional "failure" is ostensibly a lack of motivation, or his willingness to remain in a passive (feminine) role. Yéno's passivity is exemplified early on in his existence when compared to his twin sister, Waura, who was apparently the most "masculine" of the embryos to inhabit the mother's womb.

At the beginning of the novel, the reader learns that Yéno's twin sister, Waura, ate the triplet who at one time shared the uterus with them. Waura preyed on this feminized embryo who "déjà à l'état d'embryon, ne supportait aucune concurrence et souffrait d'un grave délire paranoïaque" (54). Waura's act is essentially Darwinian. To assure her survival and acceptance by her mother, Waura consumes the weaker element, simultaneously providing her with extra nourishment and doing away with a potential competitor for her mother's love and affection. Though Yéno is present during this event, he does nothing to stop his sister from consuming the weaker element, nor does he consume it himself. The dynamics of Waura and Yéno's relationship are established at this point, and Waura's tendency to dominate Yéno persists throughout the novel. Thus, Yéno is doubly-feminized: first, as a result of passive relationship with his sister, and second, because of his career choice.

Yéno's choice to become a mid-wife was a highly personal one, informed by his problematic past with his mother. As he explains, his job is a form of therapy.

> "J'accouche les femmes qui on du plomb dans le ventre. Quand une femme enfante avec moi, j'ai l'illusion de rejouer mon passé; la tête du bébé paraît, et je me vois au même âge: ma nassiance de déroule sous mes yeux…L'enfantement est pour moi une sorte de rite qui me ramène à mes origines, sauf que je voudrais changer l'histoire." (Bessora7)

On a political level, by choosing to be a sage-femme, Yéno performs a "dés-identification" that supports the notion of "les multitudes queer":

"Dés-identifications," (pour reprendre la formulation de De Lauretis), identifications stratégiques, détournement des technologies du corps et dés-ontologisations du sujet de la politique sexuelle, telles sont quelques unes des strategies politiques des multitudes queer." (*Preciado* 21)

He takes the role of sage-femme out of a strictly feminine space and appropriates it as a way in which to sort out his complicated past.

Rehearsing Sexuality: Yéno vs. Modeste

Yéno's difference is further emphasized by his brother-in-law (ironically named Modeste). Modeste, a successful gynecologist, serves as a powerful, hyper-masculine foil to Yéno's feminized, asexual persona. Modeste is quick to indicate that, as a doctor, he is capable of curing and is thus productive in society. He continually proves his "productivity" but serially impregnating the mid-wifery and nursing staff at his and Yéno's place of employment. Yéno, a midwife, can only assist in delivering babies and make the mothers' experiences more comfortable. Thus, he is a feminine caregiver, the opposite of Modeste's "puissant," masculine force.

Aside from their social/professional personas, the main sexual difference between Modeste and Yéno is the way in which each "rehearses" his sexuality. By impregnating Waura and others, Modeste proves his virility time after time. If, like gender, sexuality is something that must be performed, then Modeste's promiscuity is a way of assuring his straight identity. Yéno, however, never engages in sexual acts in the novel. In fact, he rarely discusses his physical attraction to men or women, unless he is fetishizing Nidale's ears (to be discussed further). As Bernard De Meyer writes:

> Son identité sexuelle est également ambivalente: alors qu'il est clairement un homme qui aime les femmes (il est vrain, d'un amour platonique le plus souvent), il montre des tendances homo-érotiques…il a quelque chose de subversif, à la fois en lui-même et dans ses nombreuses metamorphoses; aussi change-t-il pour un oui ou un non, comme son prénom (à l'anglaise) pourait le suggérer. (21)

As De Meyer indicates, Yéno's constantly shifting sexuality, which is never rehearsed and thus never classifiable, renders him a subversive element in a Cartesian society that privileges clarity and organization. Yéno's ambivalent bisexuality is decidedly postmodern, according to Ken Plummer's study on stories of sexuality. He states that unlike their linear and unified modernist counterparts, postmodern sexual stories are full of indeterminacies, multiple possibilities, and changing or blurring identities. It is this second category that best applies to Yéno. In his transgression lies the possibility to overcome negative stereotypes that have been imposed on him and to move beyond binary constructions of gender and sexuality toward a more fragmented, liberated sense of self.

Normative Health and Fragmented Relations

Not only is Yéno's identity fragmented and ambiguous, his mother's is as well. Throughout the novel, he maintains a conversation with "Utérus chéri," a corporally, temporally, and spatially fragmented representation of his mother who left him and Waura at birth. His conversations with this fragmented entity are the only ways in which he is able to come to terms with his own anger and sense of abandonment. Throughout the novel, he poses series of questions to Utérus that are never answered, thus augmenting his sense of separation from her and from any "normal" model of a parent-child relationship. Yéno's communication with Utérus is rendered even more problematic as a result of his polarized emotional stance. Utérus is at once loved and hated, sought after and scolded:

> "Vous nous avez pondu comme on commande le café: 'deux bébés et l'addition. Même pas s'il vous plaît. Ni merci. Ni au revoir. L'addition, je la paye encore. Et avec le pourboire,' reproche-t-il à l'Utérus aimé et haï à la fois" (Bessora 32)

In *Gender Trouble*, Butler critics they ways in which Freudian "grand narratives" privilege certain stories or patterns of identifications that supposedly produce a unified gendered self. As Freud claims, the primary element necessary for forming a (gendered) self is the relationship one has with one's mother and father (the secondary relationship would be that with one's siblings). Butler contests this idea, and develops the notion that gendered subjectivity is instead a "history of

24

identifications, parts of which can be brought into play in given contexts and which, precisely because they encode the contingencies of personal history, do not always point back to an internal coherence of any kind." (Butler 331). This applies directly to Yéno, considering the fact his mother left him at birth and played a minor role in his "gendered" development. His interactions with his sister and Modeste greatly inform his conceptions of gender and, in turn, his internal "conversations" with his fragmented mother.

His mother's abandonment engendered a series of "illnesses" or "paranoia" in Yéno, adding further to his feminized persona. In Western medical terms, the "conversations" Yéno holds with his mother would be diagnosed as mental illness. In addition, Yéno blames his inner-ear condition on his mother's absence. His sense of separation from society and exclusion from all "normal" categories of male identity is heightened by a birth defect resulting in his "acouphène mélancholique," a continual static in his right ear that transforms normal words into incomprehensible sonic transmissions resembling surrealist sound poetry.

The only temporary cure he has found to deal with the symptoms of his condition is to constantly eat raw carrots. This necessitates his leaving crucial situations both at work and in his personal life to attend to his auditory maladies. As a result, he is unable to engage in a "healthy" romantic relationship with Nidale or anyone else for that matter. In addition, because of his own hearing problems, Yéno becomes obsessed with babies' ears as well as Nidale's. He develops what would be termed as "unhealthy" obsessions and fetishes that distract him in his work, during his time with Nidale and with his political group, "La ligue des sage-femmes révolutionnaires." However, he can never be fully cured of his ear problem, since it is what permits him to achieve the desired unification with Utérus. It serves as a translator, connecting Yéno with his disembodied mother and simultaneously separating him from the rest of society.

Yéno and "les multitudes"

As a result of these myriad "abnormalities," Yéno is unclassifiable according to the limiting categories for gender, sexuality, and health imposed by the French nation. He is the ultimate "Other," an outsider, a marginalized figure. However, to leave a reading of *Deux bébés et l'addition* at this simplistic conclusion would be to deny the work of its social relevance and transformative power. Reading Bessora's novel in conjunction with Preciado's theory "les multitudes queer," one realizes that Yéno is a literary example of Preciado's "abnormal ones." Yéno's character is the result of myriad lived experiences and associations that have shaped his gender and sexuality. Returning to Butler, Yéno's particular performance of his gender does not rely on his identification with one sex or one object (i.e. his mother, Waura, Modeste). Rather, his gender is composed of a set of internalized signs, imposed on his psychic sense of identity. Therefore, his gender identity is fragmented, mutable, and constantly subject to further exterior influence.

In many ways, Preciado picks up where Butler left off. Taking the notion that "in [gender's] very character as performative resides the possibility of contesting its reified status." (Butler "Performative Acts" 520), Preciado theorizes ways in which "the multitudes" are capable of undoing fixed categories of gender and sexual performance. As she makes clear in her Manifeste contra-sexuel, Preciado bases her work on the notion that sexuality is something we "put on," in the postmodern sense, something that can be traded, commodified, and altered. In this way, she undoes the very categories that create marginalized subjects and restores power to those who cannot be contained by received definitions of gender and sexuality.

Preciado states that multiplicity is not "Otherness," since the latter would imply simply going against a hegemonic norm (and thus still adhering to these fixed systems of definition). Instead, "les multitudes" aim to proliferate the notion that in order to completely subvert the traditional institutions (which aim to be sovereign and universal), one must necessarily oppose the sexopolitical, straight epistemologies that still dominate scientific discourses on sexuality. As Preciado states, the multitudes are not simply transgressive, since this would imply alterity and marginality. Their goal is to reorganize these systems of knowledge (and the cultural definitions they produce) in order to undo the binaries between states of normalcy and alterity, thus doing away with the phenomenon of marginality all together. Yéno is representative of a member of "les multitudes" since he not only surpasses dominant systems of categorization (through his career, sexuality, and health), but also disrupts the notion of fixed gender identity that produces these categories. Such literary representations of "les multitudes" are significant on a very quotidian level in that they bring "abnormal" characters like Yéno into public focus, presenting them not as "queer," but as individuals attempting to come to terms with their own psychological problems and familial situations.

Through Yéno, Bessora appropriates the systems of knowledge that create "difference" and subsequently subverts them to call into question what constitutes "normalcy" and "deviancy" in terms of race, sexuality and gender specifically within the French context of immigration. Through the creation of protagonists such as Yéno, Bessora joins the "French" multiplicity of voices that protest against normative identitarian constructs and beyond that, open up new discursive terrains for identity articulation through literary representation.

Issues

Chapter 2

Gender Conflict in African Literature

O.Jegede

THE ambiguous portraiture of female characters by some male writers and the phallic nature of men's writings has been a matter of concern to female writers in Africa. From Elechi Amadi's sympathetic portraiture of Ihuoma in *The Concubine*, to the cowering wives of Okonkwo in Chinua Achebe's *Things Fall Apart* and more realistic portraits by Ngugi Wa Thiong'o, Sembene Ousmane, Ola Rotimi and Ayi Kwei Armah, the story keeps changing (Kolawole 94). At the early stage, in the African literary scene, most male writers were too preoccupied about themselves to remember women while the few writers like Cyprian Ekwensi presented them in negative images as prostitutes, mistresses, mothers and docile wives incapable of any intellectual exercise.

This essay is based on the premise that the battle against the misrepresentation of women is not a battle of the genders as the attempts made by male and female writers in Africa at countering traditional stereotypical representation of women have confirmed this position. It looks at two female writers whose portraiture of women contrast in two of their writings. In *The Beggars' Strike*, Aminata Sow Fall unwittingly portrays women in less than positive light. It is observed that her attempt to counter previous misrepresentations of women, to a large extent, re-emphasizes the female stereotype by giving voice to the various opinions and oppressions men perpetuate in society. On the other hand, Ify Osammor's portraiture of women in *The Triumph of the Water Lily* puts forward a positive picture of modern African womanhood. Explicating the selected novels implies our criticism of writings which demean the value and intelligence of women and calls for more positive portraits which will counter previous misrepresentation of women.

In *Womanism and African Consciousness*, Kolawole articulates various portraits of women by male writers. While condemning Wole Soyinka's ambivalence, she applauds Akinwumi Isola's and Ola Rotimi's positive female characterization among others. She insists that some women writers portray women in more derogatory images than men and advises that battle lines should not be drawn between the genders.

The need to counter these layers of distortion and misrepresentation has given impetus to diverse reactions from women writers. Women writers have made attempts at writing back, correcting and negotiating such portraits and presenting a better image of women. Their writings, in the last two decades, have countered misrepresentations and recreated the image of womanhood in different ways. Thus more women writers and critics are trying to upstage the gender codes that have promoted male domination of the power structure and its representation in literary works. Explicating the novels of Buchi Emecheta, Mariama Ba and Aminata Sow Fall, Aduke Adebayo praises the efforts of these writers for rejecting the roles of "slaves, wives, mothers and mistresses" (53) which society had designed for them.

A reading of both Aminata Sow Fall's *The Beggars' Strike* and Ify Osammor's *The Triumph of the Water Lily* shows how the authors interrogate the marriage institution, counter the misrepresentation of the woman and show some of the options available to her. Helen Cousin's discussion of marriage in fiction in the essay "Submit or Kill Yourself...Your Two Choices" focuses on more common representations of "wives who find that they cannot remain in marriages without equality and autonomy" (106). However, *The Beggars' Strike* and *The Triumph of the Water Lily* provide alternatives to the issue of oppression in marriage.

The Beggars' Strike is Fall's second novel; it is a story of conflict, selfishness, abuse of office and marital acrimony. At the centre of these is Mour Ndiaye of the Department of Health and Hygiene mandated to clear the streets of beggars who roam and harass innocent citizens. They had constituted a menace to the economy of the fictive Republic:

> ...white people especially, are beginning to take an interest in the beauty of our country. These people are called tourists you know in the old days these white people came to rob and exploit us, now they visit our country for a rest and in search of happiness. (17)

In executing this assignment, Mour Ndiaye and his department engage in a serious conflict with the beggars who remain adamant until one of them is crushed on the streets. The department succeeds, through the use of force, in evacuating the beggars from the streets. Not long after, Mour nurses the ambition to become vice president of the Republic. His marabout, Kiki Bokoul, advises him to slaughter a bull and divide it into seventy-seven portions which must be distributed to battu-bearing beggars. This leads him to make frantic efforts at bringing the beggars back. Mour requests Keba Dabo, his assistant, to do this. Keba refuses because Mour's personal interest conflicts with national interest. Mour therefore personally tries to bring the beggars back on the streets, and in the conflict that ensues, the beggars outmanoeuvre him. This shatters Mour's dream.

Ironically, the same fact of the beggars' disability becomes their source of power. Rather than roam and beg for their needs, they now accept gifts by their own terms. The leader of this group is Salla Niang, a woman "with plenty of guts" (Fall 8). From this setting and portraiture of Mour at work, the novel provides the necessary background for the portraiture of Mour at home. The story continues as Mour's political ambitions create more tension and conflict at home. However, the home setting serves as the launching pad for an x-ray of women in polygamous marriage settings.

The novel reflects the imbalances between men and women -such imbalances that may occur about selecting who to marry and how to remain married. The author presents women characters some who are able to overcome stereotypes and others who are not. The three prominent female characters in the novel are the women in Mour's life: Lolli, Sine and Rabbi. They contest their stereotyping in different ways, and exhibit different levels of consciousness: Lolli, his first wife is the submissive, passive, self-sacrificing woman who negotiates, but could not overcome stereotyping, while Sine his second wife is the radical, modern wife who refuses stereotyping. Rabbi his daughter is an unmarried revolutionary with lots of ideas.

The Beggars' Strike portrays the man as the sole authority in marriage. Mour dictates the social roles of his wives and tries to silence and confine them. Polygamous marriage is presented in this novel as a way of establishing men's authority over women, constraining the movement of women and ensuring man's easy movement in the harem. Lolli, the first wife has been married to Mour for twenty four years and all through the years, she "wore herself to a shadow to keep the home going decently on the smell of an oil rag" (31). Like a typical African woman she carries the "burden of the family's survival much more than is generally appreciated" (Kolawole 29). She is relegated to the traditional domestic sphere. When Mour's economic position improves and he is economically empowered, he takes another wife called Sine. When Mour informs Lolli, about his decision to marry another wife, the initial disappointment and shock exhibited by her are expressed in this verbal invective:

What! And you tell me to keep quiet into the bargain you ungrateful wretch! You bastard! You liar! You

34

want me to shut up, do you! Twenty four years of marriage! You were nothing, nothing but a miserable beggar! And I worked my fingers to the bone, and now you want to share everything you've got with another woman, thanks to my patience and my work, and everything that you got since with my assistance. You ungrateful wretch! You guttersnipe! You liar! You men are all the same, Guttersnipe! Shameless creature! Oh!… I should have suspected this. (31)

Mour's attempt to silence his wife even when she hurts is part of the attempt to make her conform to the passive and submissive stereotype of a wife; and is also part of the misconceived idea that men shape discourse. Being vocal and able to give expression to one's feelings and emotions as Lolli tries to do is a means of resisting oppression. As it is also seen, Lolli's productive labour is not appreciated. With her husband showing blatant insensitivity to her contributions in the relationship, she feels 'used', 'dumped' and frustrated. However, after days of frustration, Lolli succumbs to pressures from family and friends. The novel emphasizes the notion that men dictate social conventions, commonly held beliefs and attitudes when Lolli's father says: "You must know that if Mour divorces you, you will be covered with shame …. Mour is your husband. He is free. He does not belong to you" (33).

The decision to remain in the marriage is not a willing choice. It is informed by the fear of rejection by society. More often than not, women who remain and tolerate unpleasant marriages do so because of what people would say. In line with William Althusser's observation we can identify family and culture as structures which control people's choices and enforce patriarchy (Barry 165). When one's choices are conditioned by culture like Lolli's, one is tricked into believing that (s)he has freedom of choice. Besides, Lolli's low level of education and economic powerlessness to our mind, are further responsible for the fear she exhibits and the decision she takes: "Rabbi, my child if I left this house today, my parents would curse me…I'd have no work, I'd be alone, and what would I do with you children" (34).

Meanwhile Mour's political status improves; his power derives from his wealth and his wife, who had stopped working because of her husband's improved wealth, is stripped of her economic power. The situation enforces her to remain in the unpleasant marriage. Her helplessness and subsequent dependency on her husband are part of the misconceptions that women are incapable of generating wealth. This power structure creates the notion that for women, marriage is the designated route to economic stability, and to remain stable, a woman must remain in marriage; whereas stability in marriage requires more than just remaining as a figure head. Thus, Lolli is trapped and constrained on all sides: socially, economically, psychologically and educationally. Mour's second wife, Sine, appears to have more freedom than Lolli. She smokes and drinks even when Mour forbids. She is a modern wife with second wife syndrome of being the husband's favorite. After asking for Mour's hand in marriage, she discards Mour's stereotyping of her and resists his feminine construct of her:

If you think I'm prepared to be stuck here like a piece of furniture and receive your orders and your prohibitions, then you're making a mistake! I'm a person not a block of wood!.. No! I'm your wife so treat me like a wife… Monsieur disappears for days on end and when he reappears its to start giving me orders! Oh! No, Mour! You can do that to your Lolli, but I'm no sheep. (95)

Sine rejects her traditional and domestic roles and thus distinguishes herself from Lolli, the conservative and dogmatic wife. The Sine/Mour relationship demystifies, disrupts, deconstructs and subverts the established male-dominant/ female-submissive dynamic which is characterized in Lolli. However despite Sine's rejections of Mour's orders, she is as unfulfilled as Lolli. *The Beggars' Strike* portrays the woman as a subject of repression, a sexual subordinate, objectified and transformed into a source of desire that alternately tempts and pleases man. It interrogates the marriage institution and confirms it to be a prison. Through Mour's daughter, Rabbi, the novel problematises the marriage mode which requires unquestioned submission.

Rabbi is a revolutionary with lots of ideals. Her ideas run counter to conventional gender construction. She is the emerging educated revolutionary woman whose ideological position contests the negative stereotyping of women. She expresses herself freely because she is educated and unmarried. Through Rabbi, the novelist, like most contemporary African writers, attempts to redefine marriage and the place of the woman in it. However, Rabbi is antagonistic and individualistic. What she advocates about marriage – divorce – has a tinge of the radicalism of western feminism. The fact that Rabbi remains unmarried makes her suggestions only idealistic. On the other hand Salla Niang, leader of the beggars, is an economically viable woman who built a house with the proceeds of her begging. She has a firm grip on her husband and other male characters in the novel, dictating the path for them to follow. This untraditional role-reversed portrait puts her in a number of competent social functions. Thus the characters in the novel are representations of different options to oppression in marriage – to be submissive, rebellious or idealistic.

On her part Ify Osammor's *The Triumph of the Water Lily* presents the woman's struggle from an African context in a rather interesting way. The novel, which is Osammor's first, celebrates womanhood within the framework of wifehood and discusses marriage with all the seriousness that is attached to it in Africa. The seriousness with which marriage is handled in the novel brings to mind the central position given to it in both Africa and in womanist poetics: a male inclusive theory that foregrounds the complementary role of men and women. This is the nucleus of African gender system. Nkem and Odili, the protagonists, have been childless for seven years after marriage. Odili's family therefore pressurises him into marrying again. A new wife named Comfort is taken for him. Nkem, the legal wife chooses to be Odili's mistress and decides to exchange her role as a wife for that of a mistress. She packs out of the home because she would "rather be that (mistress) than a derelict and pitiful wife who is left home dejected and embittered and only in possession of the wedding ring and not the man himself" (11). Unlike Lolli, Nkem negotiates her value. To her, being a mistress is more valuable than being an abandoned wife. Nkem's decision which she believes will enhance her position with Odili and his family is a reaffirmation of some of the misconstrued portraits by writers. Despite Nkem's decision, nothing changes between her and her husband. They remain very much in love with each other (13). Nkem is left to make this choice and give her husband the freedom to satisfy what she considers to be an important need such as childbearing; 'a need which society deems 'fundamental' (17) since childlessness is a dilemma for a woman because as Emecheta sardonically puts it a "woman without children is nowhere"(Mineke Schipper 191). In Osammor's *The Triumph of the Water Lily*, as in Fall's *The Beggar's Strike*, plural marriage and childlessness are problematised and universalized: "Marriages get arranged and annulled by families for political and socio-economic reasons and not merely for love. Concubines are arranged to produce heirs if the woman taken in wedlock is unable to beget any" (11).

Osammor interrogates traditional beliefs about marriage and childlessness in marriage. Through the Nkem/Odili relationship, she shows that love in marriage is crucial for childbearing. Despite her childlessness, Nkem is still endeared to Odili. She is treated with love and respect and given fair hearing in the relationship. The plan to get another wife for Odili was told Nkem by Odili's stepmother, Mama Asaba. Not long after, Comfort gets pregnant and Nkem is shattered by the news. This creates a personal crisis to which Odili and Effua, her friends, quickly respond to. Comfort loses the pregnancy and Odili reunites with his wife. Shortly after this, Nkem gets pregnant, travels abroad and later gives birth to a baby boy; experiencing motherhood as a possible and profound role. Performing her reproductive role gives her much satisfaction.

One can infer that although Nkem had been through so many crises and emotional upsets, she still manages to overcome them with courage and grace. The author seems to say that the battles of life are enormous and only the courageous can win. The water lily is the metaphor for Nkem and every woman. Osammor re-emphasizes the importance of motherhood and mothering as necessary steps to marital fulfilment and means to "female identity formation" (Bungaro 67). The climax of the story is when Nkem falls ill and later dies. This stylistic subversion of the stereotype image of the 'mother as carrier of life and eternal nurturer' (69) introduces further tension in the narrative. In pursuance of the author's systematic womanist agenda in the novel, she makes Effua, Nkem's friend view marriage with seriousness. Effua agrees that to reach her fullest potential as a woman, she needs a man: "Marriage is a very serious business Norman, and I would very much want it to last. That is why I want you to please give me some time" (17).

Having lost her childhood sweetheart during the civil war, she is emotionally upset and careful about choosing another partner. When she meets another man who captures her emotions, she takes her time before entering into any relationship with him. The novel reveals that marriage requires commitment and understanding. Her female characters make their choices without being pushed around by men. They are career women who combine many roles. Being a career woman and a responsible wife, friend, daughter and mother are possibilities that the novel emphasizes. For instance, Effua is a successful journalist and so also is her fiancé Norman. Norman even works on the presidential team. Both characters treat each other with respect and love. They relate first as human beings and then as man and woman on equal basis. This underscores the point made by Kolawole that African womanism cannot be separated from humanism. Rather, it seeks to enrich the "female gender through consciousness raising while giving a human touch to the struggle for the appreciation, emancipation, elevation and total self-fulfillment of the woman in positive ways" (204). The female characters in *The Triumph of the Water Lily* are admirable and are as competent as their male counterparts. They are what Lolli in *The Beggars' Strike* is not: educated, exposed, and working professional and wealthy women. These qualities enable them to take control of their situation and create the space within which they operate and make choices which affect their lives and those of others. They are liberated and fulfilled individuals who assert power and are sources of liberation -extending freedom to those around them. Indeed the robust portrait of the Effua/Norman and Nkem/Odili relationships stands to correct the African world view of male heroism that is presented by male writers and Aminata Sow Fall in The Beggar's Strike.

Contemporary Nigerian female writings have clearly marked paths of raising African feminine consciousness and resisting any reality that affects or undermines the

41

humanity of women. Thus women become vocal and active arbiters of change; speaking of their gender and to their gender thereby creating a world that is devoid of gender boundaries, one in which people relate as human beings, respecting the views and feelings of one another. While Fall's Lolli and Sine struggle for space and voice, Osammor's characters are visible and audible. Osammor's fiction re-defines and restores the image of women. As she portrays the woman as an agent of change, she refuses the claim that the woman is silent and invisible. These contrastive representations of the modern womanhood by the two female writers seems to justify the opinion expressed by Kolawole that the battle against misrepresentation of women is not necessarily a battle of the genders as some women writers are more ambivalent than men. Fall does not clearly and fully portray women in positive light and her attempt to counter previous misrepresentations of women to a large extent re-emphasizes female stereotypical portraits

Chapter 3

Gender and African Modernity

O.Ojeahere

In her article, "Sisterhood: Political Solidarity between Women," bell hooks explains that the concept of "sisterhood" was a development that was fundamental to the idea of "common oppression" (396) developed by feminists. According to hooks, because the female group is oppressed, women need to work against the conditioning of patriarchy. She writes:

> Male supremacist ideology encourages women to believe we are valueless and obtain value only by relating to or bonding with men. We are taught that our relationships with one another diminish rather than enrich our experience. We are taught that women are natural enemies, that solidarity will never exist between us because we cannot, should not, and do not bond with one another. We have learned these lessons well. We must unlearn them if we are to build a sustained feminist movement. We must learn the true meaning and value of sisterhood. (396)

hooks points out that because of differences and implicit or explicit discrimination in terms of race and class, the women's movement in the US has failed to present a united front. She suggests that for these women to unite and achieve their goals, they need to struggle to overcome these divisions within their own ranks.

Implicitly responding to hook's argument in "Beyond Gender Warfare and Western Ideologies: African Feminism for the 21st Century," Anthonia Akpabio Ekpa acknowledges that as with US feminism, the concept of African feminism aims to provide woman with a sense of self-identity. While she admits that feminism in Africa is yet to be fully received, but asserts, "if practiced with an African bias and respect for African values, feminism promises to be enlightening and acceptable as its tenets prove" (31). She suggests that attention also needs to be given to the strengths of women's lives that have not particularly been highlighted by writers. "Rather than promote the stereotype of the antagonistic woman," Ekpa suggests, "writers must explore co-operation, love, assistance, and understanding among women" (35). For Ekpa, then the difficulty of achieving pan-African feminism is not so much embodied in disputes between race and class, but rather in the presentation of woman by feminists.

Despite the hurdles these critics see as confronting feminism today, both hooks and Ekpa seek ways of advocating for women's rights in order to improve women's condition through unification of the women's movement. Chinua Achebe's novels *No Longer at Ease* and *Anthills of the Savannah* may be seen as seeking this same end considering the way his female characters have fared in their relation with one another and in society more generally. This paper reveals that, in terms of gender, Achebe points at modern colonial lifestyles as offering only a veneer of older cultural values, arguing, in chorus with women like Ekpa and hooks, that in order to fight the seemingly oppressive structures that have traditionally discriminated against them, women must disregard their diversity and embrace unity. By their solidarity and unity, women can resist the powerful conditioning of patriarchy.

In *African Politics in Comparative Perspective* Goran Hyden discusses the patterns of conflict, and reveals two types: manifest and latent conflicts. He explains that there are human casualties in manifest conflicts because of its fierce nature, but says that is not the case with latent since they are "hidden in societal cleavages" (191). Hyden goes on to say that vertical and horizontal cleavages are the categories of societal cleavages. While he claims that religion, race, and ethnicity are the fundamental reasons for vertical cleavages, he asserts that the desire for economic manipulation of resources results in horizontal. Thus he reveals that "class" can be traced to horizontal cleavages (191). The fascinating thing is that this description of conflict is prevalent in Achebe's two narratives where his characters are immersed in both types of conflicts. The affinity of his characters will show the different classes these females belong to and perhaps how these conflicts impact their lives.

In examining the two stories, it is evident that the central female characters of the two novels, Clara and Beatrice, are depicted to play active roles in the lives of their men. They are the backbone of their male counterparts, making crucial decisions in the face of difficulty and misfortune, and assume responsibility for such resolution even when their men are incapacitated. Both are part of the professional working-class, and depicted as independent, a change from the usual domestication of women who are reliant on their men. While Clara is an Assistant Nursing Sister in a government hospital, Beatrice is an Assistant Secretary in the Ministry of Finance. Both are educated abroad and have foreign degrees: Clara studied nursing in England. Beatrice has a first-class honors degree in English from Queen Mary College, University of London. Both are strong-minded: Clara makes a decision to finally severe her relationship with Obi when it dawns on her that he is too weak to stand up to his parents. Likewise Beatrice refuses to play the subordinate role that Sam, the President, expects her to play to the American journalist. Both are fiancées: Clara is Obi's fiancée. Beatrice is Chris' fiancée. Both are supportive, thoughtful, and take initiative: Clara loans Obi her money; Beatrice tries to reconcile three warring friends: Ikem, Chris, and Sam.

However the portrait we see of the other female characters, Hannah, Agatha, and Elewa reveals the different class structures of these women. Hannah is semiliterate; she can read so she must have had a bit of the village-missionary education considering the historical period of her time. She is a wife and mother, loves Obi her child, loves story-telling as we see in the folktale she tells Obi, is a no-nonsense woman, as she demonstrates when she kills the village priest's goat when it eats her yams. And she is a zealous and devout woman in her faith –one of the converted female Christians in Umuofia. Agatha, on the other hand, is single, illiterate (nothing much is disclosed about her education), maid to Beatrice and therefore presumably of a lower class, and she is religious – given the picture of her preaching acts and church attendance. Elewa in her own case is semiliterate, is a sales girl, and oversees a lower-class stand as the daughter of a market woman who lives in a one-bedroom apartment. She is also Ikem's girlfriend and eventually mother of his child.

Achebe's *No Longer at Ease* demonstrates the conflict that women must overcome in addressing both gender and class disputes through the clash of personalities represented by Clara and Hannah. Clara and Hannah are the dominant people in the life of Obi, Achebe's male protagonist, and they belong to different class structures. While Clara is a symbol of the modern woman, Hannah represents duty to tradition. Obi is described as a young man who has a bright future ahead of him. But because of a bribery accusation, he appears before a magistrate to answer the allegation. As S.A. Khayyoom notes, "the novel is not about the crime, but about the compelling circumstances that lead to Obi's fall" (61). But at the moment when Obi appears to answer these accusations, neither of these female protagonists plays an active role in his life, as his mother has passed away and Clara has left his life. The narrator explains that these "two events following closely on each other had dulled [Obi's] sensibility and left him a different man, able to look words like 'education' and 'promise' squarely in the face" (NLAE 2). Without traditional Umuofia, represented by his mother, and modern woman, represented by Clara –

indeed without the presence of women altogether-- there are no complications in the ideal of education and promise. In *An Introduction to the African Novel: A Critical Study of Twelve Books*, Eustace Palmer comments on "Achebe's social concern and his terse, ironic, lucid, unpretentious style. His scintillating wit, which is itself the index of his objectivity and maturity of outlook, is everywhere apparent" (71). Indeed through Achebe's "objectivity," the variance in class and gender is depicted in the use of satire. Hannah's life reveals a glimpse of the role of the woman in traditional Igbo culture and her reason for opposing Obi's proposed wedding plans. When Obi goes to the village to see his parents, their reaction to news of his impending marriage to Clara is unsurprising given their different castes within Ibo tradition. Even for Obi's father, the idea is simply ridiculous. He explains what the consequences of Obi's action might be:

> Osu is like leprosy in the minds of our people. I beg of you, my son, not to bring the mark of shame and of leprosy into your family. If you do, your children and your children's children unto the third and fourth generations will curse your memory. . . . You will bring sorrow on your head and on the heads of your children. Who will marry your daughters? Whose daughters will your sons marry? Think of that my son. (NLAE 133-34)

As John Njoku also points out, the issue of Osu is one of social stratification which has been defined by scholars as "a cult slave, a living sacrifice, untouchable, an owner's cult, a slave of the deity, a sacred and holy being" (33). We notice that none of the arguments Obi employs can persuade his father to accept his choice of a wife. A social boundary between the supposedly freeborn and the outcast exists so they cannot mingle. For Isaac to have been adamant about the subject –which would seem to contradict the supposed "democracy" of his adopted faith– shows the seriousness of the issue. And yet Obi predicts this reaction.

For Obi, Hannah's reaction is more shocking than that of his father. David Carroll notes in Chinua Achebe that the "instinctual opposition of [Obi's] mother is more disturbing even than that of his father because it cannot be explained and discussed" (83). Hannah thinks Obi's marriage to Clara would signify the end of her life, especially because she believes she and Obi have a special relationship. She tells Obi that his marrying an outcast and bringing disgrace upon the family would be unbearable for her. It is a wonder why she, who has always been more open-minded, eager to blend cultural traditions with new ones, is even more unwavering about his intended marriage than his father. We also wonder if the woman has found an avenue to exercise her own power, which perhaps has been denied her by her husband and the community. For instance, Achebe offers us a glimpse into this oppression when Obi is at home with his parents, and the entire family gathered together for prayer:

> Obi's mother sat in the background on a low stool. The four little children of her married daughters lay on the mat by her stool. She could read, but she never took

part in the family reading. She merely listened to her husband and children. It had always been like that as far as the children could remember. She was a very devout woman, but Obi used to wonder whether, left to herself, she would not have preferred telling her children the folk-stories that her mother had told her. In fact, she used to tell her eldest daughters stories. But that was before Obi was born. She stopped because her husband forbade her to do so. (NLAE 57-58)

Even Obi suspects that Hannah has been deprived of what she enjoys to dutifully serve her husband. Her subservient role in her home may account for her using her power against Clara, even threatening suicide should he proceed with his plan. Hannah's action is indeed baffling because one would have thought that, as a woman, she might be more understanding and accommodating, and would be willing to find a common ground of agreement in welcoming Clara into the household —especially because of the seemingly oppressive position of women in her society. But Achebe's point is that oppression begets oppression: when an opportunity arises for Hannah to use what little power she possesses, she employs it as a weapon to oppose Clara, a woman like herself, instead of turning against the system that has oppressed her. Her goal to uphold this Umuofia tradition is not necessarily the right action, but she sees Clara as the only one over whom she can exercise her dominance, an opportunity rarely afforded her. In Hannah's attitude, we perceive in Umuofia's traditions race hierarchies, caste hierarchies, and gender hierarchies –all of which are repressive, and all of which reinforce the others.

We observe these repressive structures when Clara and Obi return home to Nigeria after their experience abroad. During their boat ride from England, when she and Obi first meet, Clara displays her nursing skills by administering medicine to her fellow travelers, (Obi among them), who are seasick. She is Achebe's symbol of modern female independence, with which Obi, with his modern European education, is initially comfortable. But as Achebe demonstrates, Clara's position changes as soon as they reach Lagos. There, she is relegated to the role of Obi's girlfriend: she cleans the house, cooks for him, and sleeps with him. Not much is said again about her professional training and Achebe focuses more on Clara as a sexual object, Obi's fiancée. It is possible that Achebe points to Clara's diminution as an example of how society determines people's behavior and attitude. Since women's positions tend to be somehow subordinate in Obi's Nigerian society, on her return home, the narrator describes Clara as conforming to traditional women's roles. With her return to Lagos, she is expected to marry for the reason that as Philomena Okeke argues "when women do not marry, regardless of their beauty or social skills, the Igbo suspect something is either wrong with the single woman herself or with her social background. They identify her as immoral, stigmatized, or simply unlucky" (241).

Achebe suggests that Clara would have been an ideal partner for Obi as she devotes herself completely to their relationship and is the only one who assists him financially and selflessly. For example when Obi is in dire need of money, she helps him by giving him fifty pounds. Initially, Obi is baffled about how Clara had saved such a large amount of money, but the narrative states that she "was reasonably well paid and she had not studied nursing on any progressive union's scholarship" (NLAE 107). Being a woman and also an Osu, Clara may not have enjoyed the privilege of a scholarship from the Umuofia union, an organization that is part of the system that eventually works to oppress Obi. Clara is made somewhat exempt from this oppression precisely because she is an outsider and a woman. And yet, this oppression may also have made her free. And though Obi is aware that Umuofia has been conditioned to repel outcasts, had he gone ahead with his marriage, he would have set a good example of fighting segregation as he had wanted to do on the issue of fighting corruption.

Certainly Igbo society is conditioned on the caste system. The beliefs of the people are seen to be deeply rooted in their culture and colonization has not altered it completely. Apart from the fact that Clara and Obi are prevented from marrying based on the caste system, marriage is perceived as much more than a union between a man and woman. In their book *Two Voices from Nigeria: Nigeria through the Literature of Chinua Achebe and Buchi Emecheta*, Lyn Reese and Rick Clarke explain that marriage

> was a contract between two extended families and was arranged, tying two descent groups economically and socially. The contract was sealed through the payment of a bride price. This was not payment for a wife but rather payment which strengthened the alliance

between the two families.... Romantic, individual choice love was not felt to be the basis for a good match. (16)

Although Obi's choice of a wife is based on romantic love, he still must seek the consent of his parents who are more concerned about their own social acceptance in society than about his happiness. Some parents specifically choose their children's partners but in situations where they do not, parents most often expect their children to marry from decent families and bring honor to their names. Toyin Falola sheds more light on this issue of marriage in *Culture and Customs of Nigeria*:

While arranged marriages have declined in importance, men and women still announce their choices and decisions to their parents and other family members with the hope that consent will be granted. Parents ask questions regarding ethnicity, town of origin, religion, and occupation to ensure that a good choice has been made. Most parents still prefer that their children marry a member of the same ethnic group as themselves. (120)

Igbo parents believe they should have a say in who their children marry. They may not impose brides or grooms on their children as they did in the past, but they express their concerns when their children decide to marry from families of which they do not approve, just as Obi's parents do in his case. As such, family background plays a key role in determining whether parents would give their consent to a prospective marriage or not.

Faced with such complexities, it could be said that in trying to solve their problems, Clara is more rational. When she initially suggests they part ways, Obi can only think, even if jokingly, that it is because he borrowed money from her. He informs her, "You don't want to marry someone who has to borrow money to pay for his insurance. He knew it was a grossly unfair and false accusation, but wanted her to be on the defensive" (NLAE 124). Obi irrationally puts Clara on the "defensive" because he believes it will be a blow to his manhood if Clara is the one who provides for him rather than vice versa. By contrast, her final step in deciding not to see him again, even though she is pregnant, reveals her as a sensible person who knows he is not man enough for her. Obi's decision that Clara should give him time to allow things to cool off exposes him as one who wants time to meet the impossible demands of both family and lover. Unable to choose, he remains weak, impotent, living in a world of fantasy. Obi fails to come to terms with the fact that it is not just his society that is still prejudiced, but he also is.

Sadly the existing structures make it impossible for Clara to solemnize her relationship in marriage. Because the society is immersed in schism, and because she realizes that Obi has been emasculated, she painfully relinquishes the relationship she has labored for and which she hopes would end in a union. For a woman who has devoted much of her time, love, and life to Obi, Clara seems to be more on the receiving end because apart from her gender as a woman, she also bears the stigma of an Osu which might make it much more difficult for her to start a new relationship, assuming she would even attempt one. Breaking an association which has involved such commitment is obviously not an easy decision for her to make. At various times we do observe she attempts to end their relationship which Obi seems to think is unwarranted. So we can understand her comments when she painfully says to Obi "You are making things difficult for yourself. How many times did I tell you that we were deceiving ourselves? ...Anyway, it doesn't matter. There is no need for long talk" (NLAE 143). As a result, we find Clara's pain to be reflected in her statement when she admits: "There is only one thing I regret. I should have known better" (NLAE 142), and "I ought to have been able to take care of myself" (NLAE 143). By extrapolation she is angry at herself for getting pregnant for Obi. To an extent we sympathize with her since she is the one who would possibly bear the shame of their act and trauma of going through an abortion. So we observe that Clara is deprived of a life with Obi, and as Palmer points out, Achebe "wishes to show that Obi's love affair with Clara is destroyed by his society's conservatism" (70). But the issue is does Achebe see her as having any possibility? Any hope? Or is it a hope only to be found because she has finally turned her back on Obi, who is no longer her "home"? Although the society might still be reserved, there is hope for Clara not just because she has left Obi, but because changes happen in societies, and Igbo society is not excluded from this.

On the basis of the foregoing, one finds the exit of Hannah and Clara from Obi's life particularly significant because this is where lies the tragedy of these women's lives and the raging conflict in Obi towards both. His reaction and feeling to their departure as we see is a combination of relief and sadness. On one hand Hannah's death is a reprieve to Obi as he could guiltily remember "her as the woman who got things done" (NLAE 165). Although he does mourn her loss, his remembrance of her in this way probably suggests that Obi might perhaps have perceived his mother as someone who had exerted too much dominance in his life. For a man who just lost a loved one, his ability to sleep soundly and his healthy appetite suggest a psychological state of depressurization. Moreover as Obi muses, "I wonder why I am feeling like a brand-new snake just emerged from its slough" (NLAE 165), as he suppresses the hard-working memory of his mother.

On the other hand, Achebe highlights Clara's exodus as a painful loss to Obi —one that shows his frailty and dependence on her. Though Clara might be seen as a loving and compassionate partner to Obi -one who, after he decided to separate from her, caused him "many anxious days and sleepless nights that he had passed through" (NLAE 156),Obi still sees her as a threat to him. Rather than be grateful that she helps with his loan, for example, he is worried about his ego, how such a loan reflects upon him. This dependence reveals him as a weak man who cannot make decisions on his own. This ambivalence is emphasized when he contacts a doctor to perform an abortion for Clara. We see that Obi briefly contemplates returning to Clara and going ahead with his plans to marry her. As the narrative goes, after dropping Clara at the doctor's office and seeing her leave with the doctor, "Obi wanted to rush out of his car and shout: 'Stop. Let's go and get married now,' but he couldn't and didn't" (NLAE 149). He gives up the chance to display that he is a man, capable of taking charge of his own affairs and starting life with Clara. The hope for a future generation dies with the abortion of Clara's pregnancy.

By contrast to Achebe's bleak assessment of his characters' future, Nigeria's future, in *No Longer at Ease*, in *Anthills of the Savannah*, Achebe's characters – especially women– find success through the spirit of reconciliation in Anthills of the Savannah. Through his female characters, Beatrice, Agatha, and Elewa, Achebe underscores the importance of putting aside our differences and deciding what role we want to play in society. These female characters as we see are of different classes and backgrounds, yet they are able to find solace in one another's support despite the political upheaval that claims the lives of the three disputing friends –Sam, the President of Kangan; Chris, Commissioner for Information and Beatrice's fiancé; and Ikem, the Newspaper Editor and Elewa's Fiancé. These women's disagreements between demonstrate that humans do have divergent perspectives that must be overcome, but in reconciling their differences, they can possess their own destinies.

It is Beatrice, an epitome of the modern woman, depicted as goddess and daughter of Idemili, who needs to define a place for herself in society, regardless of social structures that still tend to be discriminatory towards women. In "The Black Woman and the Problem of Gender: An African Perspective", Ali Mazrui examines sexism from different angles: benevolent, benign, and malignant. He defines benevolent sexism "as a form of discrimination which is protective or generous towards the otherwise underprivileged gender" (211), benign as a sexism that "acknowledges gender differences without bestowing sexual advantage or inflicting a gender cost" (214), and malignant as the "most pervasive and most insidious" because it "subjects women to economic manipulation, sexual exploitation and political marginalization" (218). These categories, especially the benign and malignant, are reflected in both Achebe's works. For instance, it is in reaction to the derogatory role that Beatrice believes Sam places her that she refuses to accept and function in the role he assigned to her as a guide to the American journalist. At first, Beatrice thinks she is invited to the party to reconcile Sam with Chris and Ikem, but in realizing what he wanted her to do, especially when she perceives that the journalist has the attention of all the men, she becomes defiant by becoming snobbish to the journalist and refusing to play the role of guide. Obviously using her sexuality to lure Sam away is not the proper approach to protest her perceived injustice and prove a point since she is reverting to the same sexuality she claims should not be used against her by behaving in an improper manner. Beatrice feels she has been misinterpreted as a person, and this misunderstanding may be due to the way people perceive her personality. As she says,

> [t]here is one account of me it seems I will never get used to, which can still bring tears into my eyes. Ambitious. Me ambitious! How? And it is this truly unjust presentation that's forcing me to expose my life on these pages to see if perhaps there are aspects of me I had successfully concealed even from myself. (AS 77)

For Beatrice to make this statement shows that she is willing to examine herself to determine if she has her own faults in order to recast her steps and correct her attitude towards others. Hyden notes that individuals often possess a combination of (vertical and horizontal) cleavages; "persons characterized by such crosscutting cleavages are more tolerant of others because they can more easily empathize with people coming from perspectives different from their own" (191). But that is not the case with Beatrice initially since she is not tolerant towards Agatha. In her relations with Agatha, for example, there is a class difference: their employer/employee relationship had remained strictly frosty. Beatrice claims:

> I made it clear to her from the start that I wasn't ready yet to wash and wipe the feet of my paid help. It is quite enough that I have to do the weekly grocery at the Gelegele market while she is clapping her hands and rolling her eyes and hips at some hairy-chested prophet in white robes and shower caps. (AS 760)

Their association shows that Beatrice fails to understand or respect Agatha's religious beliefs and does not attempt to make any compromise. But a fascinating twist to the novel is what is depicted in Agatha's case, that is, her antagonism toward Elewa who stays with Beatrice after the demise of Ikem. Agatha's reaction is also surprising. It is in reaction to their class structure that Agatha feels she is justified in serving Elewa a meal that befits someone of her social class. Beatrice's thoughts give us a glimpse of Agatha's character:

> After the first surge of anger Beatrice found herself feeling for the first time for this poor, desiccated, sanctimonious girl something she had never before thought of extending to her – pity. Yes, she thought, her Agatha deserved to be pitied; this girl who danced and raved about salvation from dawn to dusk every Saturday, who distributed free leaflets (she had once even sneaked up to Chris when Beatrice stepped out of the room and given him one). Yes, this Agatha who was so free with leaflets dripping with the saving blood of Jesus and yet had no single drop of charity in her own anaemic blood. (AS 168)

Someone who devotes most of her time attending church services and preaching the gospel might be expected to show the tenets of her belief, that is, to show love and kindness. Yet the hypocritical Agatha maltreats Elewa, a woman who just lost a loved one and who is in need of love and compassion. So we do understand when Beatrice berates and calls her "a very stupid girl and a very wicked person" (AS 167). She is "stupid" in the sense that she is contradicting herself by failing to reach out to Elewa and indeed deserves "pity" because she fails to bond with Elewa. Despite these discrepancies in class and perception, Achebe insinuates that even in the midst of chaos, differences, and oppression, women can still find a common ground, a link to bind them. And it is at this juncture that Elewa's character comes in to play. She brings about the spirit of reconciliation, effected through the sudden death of her fiancé, Ikem, and in the birth of her baby girl, Amaechina, whose name is a masculine one that means "May-the-path-never-close" (AS 206). Elewa is a sales girl, who lives in the ghetto with her mother, a fish seller. But she is Ikem's girlfriend; a man – the editor of the reputable newspaper, National Gazette, to be precise – who overlooks the bridge of the social division to date a girl of Elewa's class. Through Elewa's relationship with Ikem, she is able to develop and maintain a relationship with Beatrice. So we see the class difference between these two women: Elewa, a woman who did not complete her education and cannot speak Standard English, and Beatrice, a woman who has a first-class degree from a foreign university, overcome through their mutual respect for Ikem. It is important to note that it is through Ikem that the question of what women want is posed. Ikem's status as a writer and political activist gives him the opportunity to advocate for the masses. But even in his role as advocate, he excludes women as we discover in Beatrice's accusation that he has no role for the womenfolk in his political agenda. Ikem sees women as useful only as a last resort for solving problems. According to Beatrice,

> In the last couple of years we have argued a lot about what I have called the chink in his armory of brilliant and original ideas. I tell him he has no clear role for women in his political thinking; and he doesn't seem to be able to understand it. Or didn't until near the end. (AS 83)

Of course Ikem does acknowledge the truth of this accusation when he says, "Your charge has forced me to sit down and contemplate the nature of oppression – how flexible it must learn to be, how many faces it must learn to wear if it is to succeed again and again" (AS 88-89). In this comment, Ikem surely serves as the voice of Achebe, and yet he insists it is the womenfolk who need to define the role they want to play in society. We see that Beatrice takes the initiative by pointing out to Ikem what his perception of women has been. Without her showing his lapse, Ikem would not have realized his error in his thinking toward women.

Moreover Achebe seems to be suggesting that regardless of class or social status, be it political, economic, or social, women need to be united in fighting patriarchy, united in carrying out our common goals. As hooks also points out, "There can be no mass-based feminist movement to end sexist oppression without a unified front – women must take the initiative and demonstrate the power of solidarity"(396-397). hooks means that there will be no modification to what we want if there is no unified front on our part. Ultimately it is because we need to act on a collective basis that we see Achebe's female characters united at the end of the novel. Because of the bonding between Beatrice and Elewa, regardless of their class, they are able to comfort each other after the demise of their men. Moreover it is because of this bond between them that Beatrice is able to perform the naming ceremony of Elewa's daughter, an event that should have been carried out by a male, Elewa's uncle. If there was no agreement on the part of Elewa to that effect, Beatrice would not have been able to conduct the ceremony. These women settled their differences within and among themselves. As we see, Beatrice takes the step to apologize to and comfort Agatha, an action she has never done before whenever she castigates Agatha. Elewa does not bear any grudge against Agatha for the inhumane way she treats her and Agatha shows her happiness by dancing herself off and leading the praise worship during the naming ceremony of Elewa's daughter.

Again if we are to go by Mazrui's explanation of benign sexism and apply it to the depiction of Beatrice giving the child a male name, could that be considered as benign sexism because Mazrui contends that "the distinction between feminine names and masculine names is still fundamentally a case of benign sexism" (215). Although gender names might seem sexist, in this case the moniker is a significant one that hopes for continued women liberation and empowerment. This depiction might be an attempt to strike a balance in gender. Because it is Beatrice rather than her uncle who carries out this function, implicitly we are given the impression that women are equally capable of playing leadership roles in the social and political affairs of their societies.

And so we are left to ask ourselves what Achebe says about women. What societal role does he ascribe to them? Achebe suggests that women are strong, reliable, and competent, and to envisage an equal place in society for women through these fictional characters. He is careful, however, not to impose his view of what this role should be. Indeed without any initiative from women, it will be difficult to pursue our goals. The end results of these women's lives are very much different. Although Hannah and Clara seem to have something in common in their love for Obi, there is no means for them to reach a compromise socially because their society is embroiled in conflict. Consequently their inability to reconcile societal barriers results in the tragedy of these lives. However we see the other women: Beatrice, Agatha, and Elewa find something to connect them together -their strength to resolve their differences and forge a common front despite the political calamity that consumes their loved ones. This solidarity is the feature Achebe captures and brings to the fore of this novel to show the love and compassion these women are able to develop towards one another.

Chapter 4

Female Writers on War

S.A.Agbor

NADINE Gordimer's *None to Accompany Me*, Yvonne Vera's *The Stone Virgins* and Buchi Emecheta's *Destination Biafra* transmit a vivid picture of the reality of war and offer an insight into its various aspects. Some aspects of the novels depict the fear and anxiety of the paralyzing violence of war in the various spheres of ordinary life: those of work and intellectual activity, private and social life. How does the majority of the people in the representative societies of the chosen texts suffer and endure their effects and search for a means of survival? The interesting question is to what extent do their common experiences of that reality bring African women writers from different ideological and social camps closer together? Do these experiences create a common ground for them, one which allows them to transcend their ideological barriers and meet for a constructive recognition of one another? How do the different races in Southern Africa and ethnic groups in Zimbabwe and Nigeria perceive the conflict and in what ways are the various spheres of their lives, their attitudes, and visions affected by it? This approach is based on the premise that conflicts and wars are not carried out in abstract political, economic, or social systems, but in the concrete lives of people because they are the perpetrators and/or victims, and it is in their bodies and souls that the most devastating effects of such conflicts are to be found.

War is one of the recurring absurdities of postcolonial African societies and the world all over. Although war is an ugly enterprise, it remains central to human history and social change. One of the significance of the African literary imagination has been its capacity for a compelling recollection of colonial, civil and ethnic (tribal) wars. Civil wars have been fought in some African societies such as Ivory Coast, Liberia, Nigeria, Rwanda, and Sierra-Leone, Somali, Sudan, Zimbabwe, Uganda and Zaire. The effect of war on human characters is quite revealing in the novels of Chinua Achebe, Ayi Kwei Armah, Nurrudin Farah, Bessie Head, Nadine Gordimer, Zakes Mda, Buchi Emecheta, Yvonne Vera, and Lesego Malepe amongst others. Using the New Historicists theory, the cultural and sociopolitical degradation which war brings and how it affects the identity of characters in Nadine Gordimer's *None to Accompany Me*, Yvonne Vera's *The Stone Virgins* and Buchi Emecheta's *Destination Biafra* are the general foci of this study.

New Historicism is important in this analysis because the selected writers critique "serious socio-economic and political turbulence of their nations. The New Historicists deal with a text from the historical and cultural conditions of its production, its meaning, its effects, and also of its later critical interpretations and evaluations (Handbook 319). John Brannigan defines New Historicism as "a mode of critical interpretation which privileges power relations as the most important contexts for texts of all kinds" (6) while Jean Howard argues that "Literature is an agent in constructing a culture's sense of reality" (25). Howard's argument falls in line with New Historicist thinking that the study of literature within the context of history helps in the understanding of literature in history. Thus the social practices and discourses that constitute the culture of a society influence the author's creative imagination. The texts although fictive become symbolic of that society to the extent that it is shaped by the socio-cultural, political, historical, economic and religious realities of the society. This approach is relevant to our study because we are examining the political and socio-cultural war pasts of South Africa, Zimbabwe, and Nigeria as reflected in the works of Nadine Gordimer, Yvonne Vera and Buchi Emecheta.

In *None to Accompany Me*, Gordimer, unlike Vera and Emecheta who are concerned with the ugly tribal and cultural conflicts master-minded by colonial influence and ethnic and civil strives, focuses on the racial war between whites and blacks and transgender conflicts in the new South African state. Okuyade observes that "to assess African literature more effectively, critics must take into cognizance that this artistic vocation is a recreation of social realities and a critique of the African condition" (170). Indeed Gordimer's, Emecheta's and Vera's novels under study recreate important historical and political realities of their nations.

War is "an actual, intentional and widespread armed conflict between political communities" (Stanford par 1), or "a state of conflict, generally armed, between two or more entities... characterized by intentional violence on the part of large bodies of individuals organized and trained for that purpose" (Britannica 3002). The Zimbabwean guerilla and Nigerian civil wars "were fought internally between rival political factions" in order to "acquire territory and resources and further" the political aim of Robert Mugabe in Zimbabwe and Hausa power hegemony in Nigeria respectively. War has arisen out of conflicts such as ethnic, racial, political, economic and religious tensions. Apartheid was an "internal war" instituted "to further the white "aggressor's leadership". Thus the rules that guide blacks in South Africa were different from those of whites. Odile Cazenave points out that "in the late fifties and early sixties, violence meant colonial violence, from repeated humiliations and denigrations to physical violence and torture for the ones resisting colonial power "(59). The civil war in Nigeria was internally fought between rival political factions. Like most wars it was "a violent way for determining who gets to say what goes on in a given territory, ...who gets wealth and resources, whose ideals prevail, who is a member and who is not..." (Stanford par.1). There are "politically controlled wars as well as culturally evolved, ritualistic wars and guerrilla uprisings, that appear to have no centrally controlling body and may perhaps be described as emerging spontaneously"(par.10). It is "a condition of active antagonism or contention between races, gender and ethnic groups".

It was the Nigerian civil war, also known as the Biafran war, fought between July 6, 1967-January 13, 1970, that inspired Emecheta's creativity in *Destination Biafra*. The civil war was a "political conflict caused by the attempted secession of the southeastern provinces of Nigeria as the self-proclaimed Republic of Biafra" ("Nigerian" Par 1). The conflict was the result of economic, ethnic, cultural and religious tensions among the various peoples of Nigeria. Like many other African nations, Nigeria was an artificial construct initiated by European powers, which had neglected to account for religious, linguistic, and ethnic differences. Nigeria, which won independence from Britain in 1960, had at that time a population of 60 million people consisting of nearly 300 differing ethnic and cultural groups (Par. 2).

The conflict between the old and the new government like that between the different ethnic groups, parallel the South African situation in Gordimer's and Vera's novels. Apartheid regime had suppressed, oppressed and silenced black South African. These traumatic experiences lead to identity fragmentation of the downtrodden. As Elleke Boehmer in Colonial and Post-Colonial Literature posits, "to give expression to colonised experience, postcolonial writers sought to undercut thematically and formally the discourse which supported colonisation – the myths of power, the race classification, and the imagery of subordination" (3). Emecheta, Gordimer and Vera represent these divergent periods through their novels.

Gordimer's *None to Accompany Me* reveals how economic conflicts lead to racial war. "There is no doubt that the colour question in South African politics was originally introduced for economic reasons" (Biko 88).

The shift in power relations creates tension in Gordimer's text. Some of the whites are not ready to relinquish power or positions and cannot bear to share their properties. South Africa remains a society deeply ridden with violence, inequality and cultural conflict. Tertius Odendaal lives in Odensville and as a white farmer "had three farms, one inherited from his grandfather through his father, one that came as his wife's dowry, and one that he had bought in the agricultural boom times of the early eighties". Mr. Odendaal electrifies his fence so as to protect his Holsteins from thieves (blacks). And as a landlord he wants to divide his lands into plots for the Blacks to rent. This is a means to exploit the blacks. Biko accentuates,

> The leaders of the white community had to create some kind of barrier between blacks and whites so that the whites could enjoy privileges at the expense of blacks and still feel free to give a moral justification for the obvious exploitation that pricked even the hardest of white consciences. (88)

Odendaal represents the ideology of white colonists in Africa and demonstrates that extreme racism develops out of the need to justify economic exploitation. Vera Stark tries to negotiate with Tertius Odendaal whose lands some blacks are squatting on but Odendaal is not pleased with this act. Vera invites him for a discussion but Odendaal refuses to speak with Vera because he believes that Vera is not a woman as he knew women (24). In the confrontation between him and the blacks, he kills some blacks and wounds many in Odensville. This conflict brings in the theme of physical violence/war as a result of racial discrimination. Consequently, he and his supporters kill nine blacks and fourteen are wounded. The novel therefore seems to be an indictment of the colonial or apartheid system, but at the same time it helps us to understand the relationship that exist between the characters' past and the present state of existence.

The various reflections on this experience by the protagonists and other characters in the novels are conspicuous.

Buchi Emecheta in *Destination Biafra* draws attention to the devastating consequences of this war on the populace and equally highlights the role women played in the war. *Destination Biafra* describes postcolonial Nigerian war society and politics in the middle of a bloody civil war caused and fueled by Western economic imperialism and resulting in genocide and economic disaster. In *Destination Biafra*, Emecheta reveals British capitalist legacy in post independent Nigeria. The dialogue between Sir Fergus Grey, Macdonald and Alan Grey is revealing (5-7). The discovery of oil in the eastern regions and the Benin areas motivates Alan Grey's capitalist quest. He states: "the whole of the eastern region and the regions around Benin ...are full of oil, pure crude oil, which is untouched and still needs thorough prospecting"(6). He wonders how they "are to hand it over to these people who've had all these minerals since Adam and not known what to do with them (6). Alan Grey convinces Saka Momoh to accept military assistance in exchange for mortgages of oil wells saying: "The whole mid-west is rich in oil; part of the break away state is very oily; I'd sign percentages of the oil revenue over to people who would help you win the war" (153). He goes to London to negotiate with the authorities of the Ministry of Defense and "two days later Alan Grey landed in Nigeria in a plane loaded with discarded British armory new trade in ammunition and human blood had began"(156) . The British colonial masters give arms to those whom they wanted to be at the leading position in the country.

Thus the coup d'etat was a war for liberation from Britain's stooges. Nwokolo, one of the agents, draws our attention to British manipulation: "I would rather say our destination is "Biafra' since as far as I am concerned we're not yet independent. We sent away one set of masters without realizing that they had left their stooges behind" (60). Alan Grey brainwashes Saka Momoh to enlist mercenaries to fight the Biafrans because it is "the best way may be to get a few white mercenaries to lead some black soldiers trained in England..." (200-201). Four West Indians: Hawkins, Ennis, Pascoe and Clemens are contracted and paid to fight both the Biafran forces. Significantly Ngugi wa Thiong'o in *Homecoming* writes that the Biafran Nigerian conflict was a war "where ordinary men and women who had not in any case gained much from Uhuru were made to slaughter one another with guns supplied by competing Western powers..." (50). He further warns that the potential of a Biafran type of conflict exists in every African country that has doggedly refused to dismantle capitalism and colonial economic structures, to correct the legacy of an uneven geographic and social development "(50). Thus "Uhuru" (independence), becomes a nightmare. The general atmosphere of constant insecurity transforms the spatial environment of South Africa, Zimbabwe and Nigeria. The citizens are constantly conscious of physical and silent dangers. Says Christopher O'Reilly in *Post-Colonial Literature*:

> Another context which informs the writings of post-colonial authors: the problems faced by independent countries and the lack of security and certainty in such a world. On one level post-colonial literature is an expression of these crises as well as testimony to those who resist them. (6)

These novels give us the opportunity to interrogate the complexities of identity negotiation, the psychological war they undergo. *The Stone Virgins* contrasts with the psychological war in post apartheid South Africa of transition as witnessed in *None to Accompany Me*.

During ethnic, civil and racial wars, women pay the higher price because their bodies become sites of violence through rape and sexual abuses seen in the quandary of Thenjiwe, Nonceba and Debbie Ogedemgbe. In her quest to unite the warring factions, Debbie accepts Odumosu's request that she should meet and dialogue with Abosi on the stalemate. Debbie sets out for the journey with her mother (Mrs. Ogedemgbe) and their driver, for the Eastern region. They meet a fierce resistance from the federal forces along the Lagos/Asaba road who strip her of her gun and uniform. Mrs. Ogedemgbe accosts the ferocious federal forces who want to sexually assault her daughter: "You want to compare my nakedness to your mothers'... do whatever you want with me, and afterwards kill me. But please, in

the name of your mother leave my daughter out of it. ..."
(133). Despite her pleas Debbie is raped by the federal
forces, an act which leaves an indelible print of trauma in
her psyche. The narrator says: "She could make out the
figure of the leader referred to as Bole on top of her, then
she knew it was somebody else, then another". Different
soldiers rape her; "pain shot all over her body like
arrows" (134). The violation is intensified as "She felt
her legs being pulled this way and that.., and Debbie lost
consciousness" (134). The normal social relationships are
destabilized and replaced with "by perverse and violent
relationships, between rapist and victim, or murderer and
victim. Fathers rape daughters; pregnant mothers abort;
returning soldiers terrorize those they have liberated"
(Gunner 3). The physical violence the federal forces
inflict on her underscores the numbness of their
consciences. Debbie emphatically tells Alan Grey; "I
mean I was raped, several times, Alan in the bush, I don't
know by how many men, I didn't count" (243). The war
has turned the men into animals. Furthermore, Lawal
rapes Debbie in the "operation mosquito" campaign,
Debbie suffers from his sexual perversion. Lawal
considers the Debbie / Alan Grey affair a treachery. He
opines: "You are still his play thing then, are you? You
are all saboteurs, selling our country to the foreign
powers. People like you! (175). He uses this anger as a
reason to rape her. He orders her "Go in, go in there. I am
going to show you that you are nothing but a woman, and
ordinary woman" (175).

Similarly in *The Stone Virgins* Thenjiwe is beheaded
and Nonceba raped and mutilated during a massacre in
Kezi outside Bulawayo by Sibaso a traumatized war

veteran. Nonceba watches her sister beheaded, before the attacker rapes her and cuts her lips. "He presses her down" (62)" as he violates her. The narrator says "He offers words that could heal. He closes his eyes and moves his lips against her neck. His words flood her ear tips... Her legs hang empty, within his parted thighs, then his legs close and hold her tight" (64-65). In this horrifying situation he asks Nonceba "Are you afraid to look at me?" Nonceba is petrified and Sibaso insists and orders her: "Hold me. Touch me here. Look at me. I said touch me here" (64). This is not a normal love exchange but a rape and he is requesting a more intimate contact. Post Traumatic Stress Disorder is seen here because for a moment he thinks he is having intimacy with a loved one which is not the case. The result is Post Traumatic Stress Disorder (PTSD), a "psychiatric condition that can develop following any traumatic, catastrophic life experience" (PSTD par.1). Nonceba describes him thus: "His name is Sibaso, a flint to start a flame" (73). Furthermore when Nonceba is in the hospital she notices that the patients murmur in their sleep. These are the murmurs of those who sleep in pain, with wounds which no one can heal because the "wounds are in their hearts. There are the wounds of war which no one can heal, bandages and stitches cannot restore a human being with a memory – intact and true inside the bone" (86). Grace Musila's observation in Vera's Without a Name and Butterfly Burning applies also to The Stone Virgins:

The violence of rape, surveillance, and poverty are first and foremost experienced at this corporeal level for many women. Under such circumstances, the

75

physical existence of the body in a sense marks a site of betrayal, as the bodies are open to manipulation by oppressive forces, to propagate the women's subjugation. (58-59)

This description aptly fits Debbie situation in *Destination Biafra*. The women war veterans in The Stone Virgins "carry this dark place in their gaze" because of the trauma and haunting realities of war (53). The social world is broken as a result of the liberation war against the colonizers and the civil war against the neocolonialists. In this wise, Liz Gunner states that:' Family, community, nation –all barely exist and, where they do, they are invariably sites of unspeakable violence and betrayal" (3).

Physical violence is an aspect of war. *The Stone Virgins* reveals the psychological as well as physical effects of war in Matabeleland. The hospital scene in *The Stone Virgins* reveals the estrangement of the patients from society. They are physically and psychologically isolated because of the memory of their assaults. The nurses treatment of the woman who becomes psychological demented after she is forced by two soldiers to kill her husband to save her two sons (78) is an instance. The husband raises his voice towards her pleading "… kill me." He was desperate to die and save his two sons". And she hatches the husband to death with the axe. It is only when "he was dead" that "the men left her in that state. A dead husband and two living sons" (80-81).

Moreover, the "expressionless" faces of the soldiers torturing Mahlatini to death is depressing just as Sibaso's beheading of Thenjiwe and raping of Nonceba is beyond human imagination. The narrator reveals that this "is not the first death he has held in his arms". He clutches Thenjiwe "like a bird escaping" (68). The body falls and he pulls "the body back, bone bright white from it, neck-bone pure, like a streak of light the bone vanishes into the stream of blood oozing out" (68). This description is horrible and registers how inhuman war can be. Another sordid nature of war in The Stone Virgins is seen in the burning of Thandabanthu Store. The Fifth Brigade soldiers "with force and intensity" yet "expressionless" faces torture the innocent owner of Thandabanthu store Mahlatini -to death with pieces of burning plastic. Mahlathini's death is crude. He never looked up at the man, at the gun, at the voice that is going to kill him. He knows and accepts that "he would never see his children again" (122). The soldiers' numbness to their atrocities is seen in the way "they tied him up (and) ... let the burning emulsion down on him. The soldiers focused on this one activity with force and intensity" (123). Witnesses say "Mahlathini howled like a helpless animal" (123). Yet he dies for a crime he did not commit. Besides, twenty customers who happen to be in the shop are shot to death (122-3). The narrator implies that instead of protecting civilians, "a multitude of soldiers are disturbing the peace of the land" (123). This war is not between races but between the ethnic groups of a nation. Thus the narrator describes the people and the soldiers as engage in "a different war in which they were all casualties" (161). The soldiers and the masses are all hurting in different ways because it hurts to get hurt.

The war does not take place away from civilian life. Lives of children women and men are affected. Homes and family lives are affected. Family units are broken. Likewise in Destination Biafra Ugoji, an Igbo from the Midwest to survive the war in the north disguises his Igbo identity through the Hausa serrations on his jaws so he can pass for a Hausa man. Ugoji escapes the northern assault against the Ibos by denying his very identity: "I am not an Ibo" (87).

This is psychological trauma as the character tries to negate his original homeland/identity in order to survive the war. He decries the incessant killings of citizens and laments on the kind of independence Nigeria has from its ex-colonisers. He comments: "When the Europeans ruled us, few people died; now we rule ourselves, we butcher each other like meat sellers slaughtering cows" (88-89). The comparison highlights the savagery and futility of man's quest for power. Olabode Ibironke argues that "the genealogy of power shows that hegemonic hierachization and abuse of power in animist/feudal Africa has formed a sub-stratum that continues to influence the use of power, position and office in Africa today" (80). Significantly, independence Ugoji reveals bring a different kind of war in post colonial Africa. In the same vein Sibaso, a victim of this political ugly history in The Stone Virgins observes: "The independence arrived and brought with it a spectacular arena for a different war in which there were casualties" (161). Paul Zaleza reveals that "Vera reinforced her image as a politically courageous writer as she unflinchingly confronted the horrific violence in Matabeleland perpetrated by President Mugabe's regime anxious to stamp its authoritarian will on the newly independent country"(14).

The physical violence of war results in psychological disturbance. Debbie's mother Stella Ogedemgbe "could not shut out the horrible way the Ibo women with the child were killed, how they had pushed the butt of the gun into her, how they had cut her open...(136). This experience shows the trauma that will always be part of the lives of war victims. War becomes debasing, it dehumanizes humans to bestial activities. Soldiers kill and loot with the only justification that "it's war time". The novels depict that for soldiers war time is the period of lawlessness, no respect of human rights and above all, a time to heed to their carnal and amoral desires. There is a general sense of insecurity.

Vera Starks in *None to Accompany Me* warns her son Adam to be aware of the world outside them because "...living here is dangerous, even this garden, this house" (254). She underlines: "If people come to rob, you can be shot or knife as well, if you walk up the wrong street and there's demonstration on, you can in hale tear-gas or get shot, you'll learn all about this" (254). The threat of violence, in its diverse forms is unpredictable. The populace is permanently conscious of these dangers and thus tries to reduce their movements to a bare minimum. The effects of war on men are quite telling. Just like the veterans in Leslie Silko's Ceremony this men idle in and around Thandabantu Store. These soldiers –Rhodesian soldiers and guerrilla sympathizers– are neither here nor there. The narrator writes that these are "...men ...who have returned from the war with all their senses intact except for that far away travelled look that makes the girls a bit dizzy, a bit fearful, a bit excited" (47). Vera describes them as "solid men" who nevertheless "wear lonely and lost looks" and "guard their loneliness,"(47). They are lost because like Tayo in Ceremony they are afflicted by recurring war nightmares (49). Anne Gagiano writes that "Sibaso may well be pictured as one among these anonymous male ex-combatants" ("Reading" 66). What is significant is that they can no longer fit into the society, hence as Gagiano notes "The female ex-combatants recognize the futility of the attempt by starry-eyed younger women to make the men who have returned from the war forget how they had to "hold [their] own screaming voice in [their] hands, to fight" ("Entering" 50). They suffer Post Traumatic Stress Disorder (PSTD) as a consequence of war. Sibaso and the guerilla fighters characterize the signs such as nightmares and detachments. Their "lost looks" symbolize feelings of estrangement and fragmentation.

The effects of war, violence coup d'état and revolution in South Africa, Zimbabwe and Nigeria is seen in family disintegration. The various forms of war affect the identity of the people, particularly children. We realize that the children also constitute another group that suffers from the oppressive forces of the war. Children suffered from diseases caused by malnutrition and sanitary problem and mortality rates were therefore high. In None to Accompany Me students in the high school are victimized, imprisoned and killed for a cause they know nothing about. This creates a dysfunction in the society because they are not opportune to go to school as kids do in normal situations. The gravity of the impact of war in education is highlighted by Gordimer. Black kids of "eighteen, nineteen and twenty years" (26) are attending primary education in post apartheid an opportunity that was denied them during apartheid. They are not given the same opportunity because during apartheid black children are chased by policemen from one place to another. Their educational life is full of disturbances; the government forces them to move from their homes to unknown areas. The frequent interruption of activities due to a sudden outbreak of violence jeopardizes continuity and efficiency. Some of them are forced to inculcate violence as necessary strategy for survival. Oupa drops out from school to join political action to fight for their right. He ends up in prison, Robben Island without finishing his education.

The trauma of war in children is seen through children characters like: Boniface, Ogo and Ngbechi. Ogo, Ngbechi's five-year old brother in his innocence expresses his belief thus: "When we get to Biafra...my father and my mother will cook us fried plantains and chicken stew..." (210). He intones: "when we get to Biafra all out troubles will be over" (210). These kids witnessed the horror of war in the death of Ngbechi. While in Asaba the women soliciting medical help from the nuns in the mission hospital for Ogo who has a dysentery attack. Ngbechi hastens to carry his younger brother Ogo to the hospital and "The observing officer's gun coughed once and Ngbechi lay on the tarred road bleeding to death" (221). Debbie, Dorothy and Uzoma leave the children in their care and run up to the soldiers, screaming: "go on, shoot all of us! Shoot us too, please shoot us!" (221). The death of the child recaptures the predicament of children during the civil war.

Significantly, many children, wives, husbands will no longer know the normal social order. Friends and relatives are lost. The family unit is destroyed. This is an indictment of military rule. One cannot help the feeling of trepidation in the atrocities lay bare. The ills of materialism, military coup d'etats cannot be applauded because they are a poor precedent for a democratic system.

Gordimer's *None to Accompany Me* also illustrates the place of land and housing in conflicts and war. In the novel, most lands and houses are owned by White South Africans. The war supposedly ends in a transitional government and many dislocated blacks still are homeless and frustrated. The political marginalization and economic strangulation fuel ethnic tensions and forces many to choose a life of exile in order to survive. These exiles also enforce various form of devastation on the victims. The exiles return with no place to call theirs. Homelessness and unemployment become a problem. Most blacks who returned from exile have no house or land of their own. Sibongile, Didymus and their daughter Mpho live in Vera's apartment after their return. The narrator informs us:

> Now communities whose removal the foundation had been unsuccessful in stalling are coming to present the case for having restored to them the village, the land, their place which was taken from them and allotted to whites. (13)

The controlled movement of African workers within the country through the natives Urban Areas Act of 1923 and the pass laws separated family members from one another as men usually worked in urban centres, while women were forced to stay in rural areas. After apartheid women take menial jobs meant for men. When Sibongile sees these women, she is surprised because she "didn't know that women did this work, now" (51). In Gordimer's novel Oupa goes to the city to seek for greener pastures. At the legal foundation he works "he is decently paid by decent standard of a foundation that provides medical care and pension fund" (53). But his "decent salary" cannot pay his rent; buy food and clothing for himself. He takes in a roommate to help with the rents but the friend "moved into the flat with him, the couple, and the two children" and "Soon this friend who had to contribute to the rent, was joined by another, workless and penniless" (57). The feeling of hopelessness is recounted by Didymus: "There were no gods for them to turn to, neither. No new state, not yet: no security that was not at the same time part of the threat" (265).

Likewise in *The Stone Virgins* the migrant workers move from Bulawayo to Johannesburg searching for a means of survival "city labourers" who "voyage back and forth between Bulawayo and Johannesburg" (12). The displacement of people as a result of war is also seen in Vera's *The Stone Virgins*. Sibaso describes how he goes to look for his father in Njube Township. The person he meets in his fathers house does not even know his fathers name and tells him a rumoured history about the person who used to live in the house, who is likely to be or not to be his father. We see that the general atmosphere of constant insecurity transforms the cities into an unpredictable and insecure environment.

The conflict between genders in war roles in Gordimer's, Emecheta's and Vera's texts is revealing. Debbie Ogedemgbe, the Oxford educated daughter of a corrupt Nigerian government minister transgresses her traditional role to take an active part in Biafra's struggles just as Sibongile in *None to Accompany Me* and the female guerillas in *The Stone Virgins*. The ZIPRA female guerrillas in *The Stone Virgins* fight alongside men in the guerrilla war. Debbie forgets her Oxford education and commands a regiment of about twenty soldiers who readily execute her commands. She and Barbara (Babs) dress in tattered army uniform and smoke just as men. Mrs. Ogedemgbe could not understand their transformation. She comments: "We all want freedom for women, but I doubt if we are ready for this type of freedom where young women smoke and carry guns instead of looking after husbands and nursing babies"(109). During the stalemate that eventually results in a civil war, Saka Momoh entrusts in the hands of Debbie a "delicate mission" because he thinks Debbie can use her "feminine charms to break that icy reserve of" Abosi (123). Debbie "neither Ibo nor Hausa but a Nigerian" (126) accepts this mission to enforce peace. So women are used as baits. She realizes that her body becomes an antiwar object: "so now men thought she could use her sexuality to make Abosi change his stand. She was to use her body because Saka Momoh did not want to get into war with the Easterners" (126). It must be noted that during war, the woman's body is seen as a site for sexual gratification. Chief Odumosu tells her: "Don't forget, my dear, that you are a woman. That is why we are giving you this delicate mission" (129).

Debbie gets to Abosi's residence and a member of the Biafran forces orders: "Shoot her'. Another soldier says: "Oh leave her, she is only a woman. What harm can she do and how could we explain to His Excellency?"(238). She finally meets Abosi who refuses to yield to the peace mission. Instead he articulates to her a woman's privilege. "If you were a man, you would have been shot this minute as a traitor. So you see, being a woman has its advantages" (240)).

In the transitional post apartheid period the woman comes to the centre of the new political arena. *None to Accompany Me* reveals the cultural conflicts between male and female roles in transgender as tactics for survival. Gordimer highlights how post apartheid offer women new opportunities in the political and economic structures in the society and how these affect their life. Vera Starks and Sibongile take the initiative to transgress their roles and step into ascribed men roles. Women like Vera and Sibongile are seen as man woman. Odendaal a rich farmer in the South African community holds that, Vera Stark "was the kind of woman who produced revulsion in him. To him, in fact was not a woman at all, as he knew women" (24). Sexually he does not find her appealing. But what he hates her most for is her effrontery in questioning him. He states "the mouth asking questions and addressing him without the respect and natural deference due to a male..." (24). Afrikaner nationalism remains a kind of image representing the abuses of apartheid. Vera Stark evolves at the beginning of *None to Accompany Me*. The narrator says. "She was working until midnight at home as well as all day at the offices" (21). At the end of the novel she is referred to as grandmother, daughter and baby (309). Sibaso recounts the aftermath of war in his soliloquies which represent the psychological trauma of war. The war affects him such that his "mind is perforated like a torn net and even falls through like a stone" (74). This causes fragmentation in his personality. "He cannot escape" from these memories because "He is the embodiment of time" (75). Sibaso's fragmentation is also seen in his despondency. He says: "My name is Sibaso" as if unsure of whom he is. Yet he has "crossed many rivers with that name no longer on his lips, forgotten. It is an easy task to forget a name" (74). The Post Traumatic Stress Disorder leads to detachment and split personality. Thus he says "other names are assumed, temporary like grief, you discard names like old resemblances and during a war we are lifeless beings" (74).This highlights that for them to be able to fit into their roles as soldiers who kill and destroy they negate their sense of thinking beings with sensibilities. Consequently, they "are envoys our live intervals of despair, a part of you conceals itself so that not everything is destroyed, only a part. The rest perishes like cloud" (74). His further fragmentation is seen when he hides on the Gulati hills during the guerrilla war, and says "I count each nameless ancestor on my dead fingers... Nehanda the female one. She protects me with her bones" (213). Driver and Samuelson state that The Stone Virgins "creates some awkwardly close connections between what (51) are often crudely defined as the 'victim' and 'perpetrator' positions" (151-52). The effect of war on him affects him psychologically. Just like Tayo in Leslie Silko's *Ceremony*, war veterans like Sibaso "wear lonely and lost looks", are "wound[ed]", "troubled" and plagued by "screaming" nightmares (75). Sibaso describes Africa as "a continent which has succumbed to a violent wind, a country with land but no habitat" (74) and "a continent in disarray"(76). Gagiano insists that "Cumulatively, the men and women who have emerged, apparently victoriously, from the sixteen-year liberation war are the manifestations of a "broken continent" (53).

The vision of Vera in this novel is seen through the way she concludes the novel. It is important that each person takes responsibility of his/ her actions and take decisions that will affect and shape their lives positively. Cephas the former lover of Thenjiwe is the contrasts of Sibaso. He assists Nonceba to "find places for herself to inhabit, without him" (165). His desire is "to help, to sustain, not to contain" (169). He is the ideal of a man. It is him who pulls Nonceba out of her nightmare. Meg Samuelson writes that "Cephas... rescued Nonceba from the landscape of trauma" (28), and is the "emblem of the new man" (28). Samuelson emphasizes that "the novel concludes with him withdrawing from Nonceba, allowing her to find her own paths through the city, her own spaces in their home" (28).

Emecheta's *Destination Biafra* ends up with Abosi failing in his crusade to secede the Eastern and Midwestern regions of Nigeria as Nigeria is "successfully handed over to the approved leader, Saka Momoh" (259). The narrator notes that "the fact that he came from the minority tribe, and had an ample supply of guns and bombs, would stabilize his position" (259). Ironically this stability is needed "to allow foreign investors to come in and suck out the oil" (259). Significantly wars have their roots in the respective cultural and political communities, where the role of the nations and citizenry is not respected appreciated and their rights to statehood aborted. It is not for the good of the populace. Indeed these texts are steeped in the socio-political and historical realities of their societies.

André Brink in "Interrogating Silence: New Possibilities Faced by South African Literature" posits that "The full effect of this burden shouldered by writers under apartheid is only beginning to come to light now that the situation is in the process of changing"(16). Brink further states that "the writer sets out to achieve, the need to function as a historian -that is, through 'reporting' and 'representing'- informed much of her/his activity and defined much of her/his scope" (17). Through these violations of human lives, we get an inner glimpse to the cruel nature of war and violence on ordinary human beings who have nothing to do with the war. Gordimer's focus in None to Accompany Me is on the nature of social and political war in Southern Africa. The multiplicity of culture, gender and class amongst the various peoples affected by the conflicts in the novel cannot be overemphasized. War is not only physical, and political but social, economical and psychological.

For Nigeria, the consequence of the civil war in present day is such that the old ethnic and religious tensions remained a constant feature of its politics. The civil war turned Nigeria into a lawless state wherein women are ruthlessly raped, men castrated and people gorged of their eyes. Emecheta's idea is that neocolonial corruption and British exploitation have led to the breakdown of social order, civil wars and the military constant seizure of power through coup d'etats. However, the women in Emecheta's text summon courage and determine to live and forge a new beginning. It is for this reason that she imbues Debbie with the decision to use part of her inheritance to provide for children who have been made orphans by the civil war. She also chooses to write and publish a novel which chastises the evils of war and power quest that happens to be the root cause of social fragmentation (195).

The role of female writers as evident in the novels under study is to conscientize the people and make each one redress their contribution in these wars as the pain and grief of lost ones cannot be forgotten. It is ever present in the absence of the responsibilities and role they played while alive. They transmit a vivid picture of that reality and offer an insight into its various aspects. The wars include ethnic tribal wars, racial wars, civil wars, gender wars, as well as verbal wars. All these wars lead to psychological and emotional trauma. Some even experience psychotic disorder and fragmentation. These writings are filled with the themes of violence and war. Here Gordimer, Vera and Emecheta fall into the category of "the intellectual as a representative figure that matters "(Edward Said 13). They have "visibly represent(ed) a standpoint of some kind" and made "articulate representations to his or her public despite all sorts of barriers" (13). These representations are the memories of wars in the past and their consequences in the present. The total life of the nation and the people are invaded and the whole world becomes a nightmare. The moral is that war should be prevented at all cost because it destroys and ruin lives and beliefs of people.

Chapter 5

Male Authority, Female Alterity

J.T.Tsaaior

IN phallocentric societies, the patrilineal principle takes precedence over the matrilineal in all civil, religious, political and cultural institutions central to societal engineering. Socio-economic structures are also ideologically patterned to privilege the phallocentric order. The political strategy is to institute hierarchies that maintain and perpetuate male ascendancy and hegemony over the female. In this asymmetrical, agonistic and (en)gendered terrain, the definition of individual subjectivity is executed essentially through the sieve of selfness and otherness. This sexist and gender-specific monad reduces individuality and refracts life and existence through gender politics and paradigms in the rigidity of maleness and femaleness without appreciating the complementarity of the two sexes.

This chapter engages male authority and female alterity in Akachi Adimora-Ezeigbo's *Children of the Eagle*, a novel which negotiates dominantly issues in the (en)gendered terrain of patriarchal Igbo society in Southeastern Nigeria. While the patriarchal tradition ideologically seeks to ensure the continuity of phallocentric culture, the matriarchal tradition advocates transition and change in the dynamic and nimble-footed world of post-modernity and globalization. We will interrogate the representation of women in the novel and show how women too have appropriated the rites of public space to tell and retell their stories to privilege their perspectives, rehabilitate their dilapidated image and affirm their humanity. By observing that women have fashioned a meta-language which they have deployed in countering male sexist and genderised delineation of women in negative and negating signifiers we implicate language and its signifying systems and codes as strategic to the deconstructive process.

Trends in Nigerian Writing

Recent trends in Nigerian writing have grappled, and will continue to grapple, with multiple and shifting issues whose mood and temperament have been governed and defined by major concerns of historical and contemporary significance. The historicity and contemporaneity of this trajectory constitute a veritable continuum that is particularly fore-grounded in the novelistic tradition. However, the trajectory is not exclusive to the novel. History and its plural conspiracies are present in the realities of the imperialist and colonialist encounter, the dissolution or erasure of a distinct traditional and cultural ethos, the nationalist ferment which inevitably culminated in political autonomy on 1 October, 1960 and the 1967-1970 civil war which stalked the 1966 maiden coup d'etat (Amuta 2). Nigerian history is also manifest in the pervasive disillusionment and disenchantment that became concomitant with the decadence of the emergent bourgeoisie building up into the post-civil war oil boom of the 1970s and the political perfidies perpetrated by a military whose ostensibly interminable interregnum, after a short spell of civilian democracy, held hostage the Nigerian nation-state in the 1980s and 1990s and reduced it to a pariah and a state in a perpetual state of becoming (12). Nigeria's contemporary existence constitutes a mosaic on which is concretely etched an amalgam of issues which underwrite a nation writhing in throes, desperate to define its ethos which, to Femi Osofisan, is at present "contradictory, agonistic and incoherent" (12). Riddled with institutionalized corruption, political turbulence, a stunted democratic process, flagrant abuse of fundamental human rights and freedoms, ethnic strife and civil conflicts, as well as a deepening social morass and official malfeasance, Nigeria's contemporary condition is a fitting testament of a failed nation-state waiting to be saved from the precincts of a gaping precipice (121).

Binaries of Tradition and (Post)Modernity

Children of the Eagle constitutes a trilogy, the Umuga trilogy, whose earlier siblings are *The Last of the Strong Ones* (1996) and *House of Symbols* (2001). The novel's interlocking, gripping and penetrating story is history, or more appropriately, herstory spanning roughly a temporal frame of four decades. Set in Igboland in south-eastern Nigeria, the novel creatively constructs or weaves a world which powerfully pulsates with tensions between tradition and (post)modernity, continuity and change and heaves with the forces of nature and culture, patriarchy and matriarchy, in an opposition of binaries and what Mary Pratt calls "asymmetrical relations" (3), each jostling for ascendancy to institute its hegemony. In a dominantly phallocentric world known for its republicanism, the novel presents an Amazon of a matriarch, Eaglewoman with her five female children, and a single male child. These include Ogonna Okwara-Nduka, a secondary school teacher in Lagoon City married with four children: two daughters and two sons; Nnenne Okwara-Okoli, a senior lecturer at the University of the South, Lagoon city, married with a son and a daughter; Obioma Okwara-Ebo, a pastor and evangelist also married with two sons and two daughters; Amara Okwara, a journalist who is single; Chiaku, a medical doctor who practices in London and the youngest, Nkemdirim, a son who is a secondary school student in Kada city. As the narrator compellingly states,

They are Eaglewoman's children. They form the centre of her life. She wakes up every morning with thoughts of them flooding her mind. Thinking of them means praying for them. She ends the day with more thoughts of them, more progress for them. Their names sizzle on her lips like bean cakes frying in hot oil, lull her to sleep every night, nudge her to wake every morning to the day's routine. They are the joy of her life since the loss of Osai, her husband. If Eaglewoman were the kind of person who painted her feelings with words, she would confess that a part of her shriveled up and died with him. The other part that is alive belongs with her children. Each morning, without any conscious effort on her part, the thought of her children animates her body, waxes it to stir, to rise with the sun. (17)

As the narrative progresses, these women (except Chiaku and Nkemdirim, the youngest and only male member of the family) gather at the grave-side of Pa Josiah Obidiegwu Okwara, the late patriarch, in silent prayer preparatory to the commemoration of his passage. This is a traditional and cultural imperative prescribed by a phallic order for family members of the deceased especially for women not only in Igboland but also other African societies. Some of these women are compelled by the contingencies and expediencies of a patriarchal ideology to undergo burial and reburial rites that are demeaning, prohibitive, and subversive and hyphenate the very humanity of women (Hay and Stitchter 44). In this male constructed and defined tradition, therefore, the father-right or patrilineal principle assumes precedence and pre-eminence over the mother-right in cultural, economic and political practices and is inscribed and codified within the contours of societal institutions. This socio-cultural engineering process places womanhood on the side of fundamental lack and inscribes the female as the other who is apportioned a limited space on the margins of mainstream, male-dominated Igbo society. It is within this agonistic knowledge and cultural schema that the male child, for instance, is indispensable in society and is preferred to the female (Chukukere 2). Against this significant backdrop, the arrival of a male child to any family is celebrated with pomp as it constitutes a monumental event whose cultural significations gravitate to the perpetuation of the family genealogy, the continuity of tradition and cultural institutions which privileges patriarchy and its ideological hegemony.

More fundamentally, the male child is the custodian of family property. This explains why Nkemdirim's birth to the Osai family is traditionally considered the arrival of the family in all cultural ramifications. Though still a minor, he is designated heir to the family landed property such that when he is in a critical condition as a result of an auto-accident, this is viewed as a potent threat not only to the continuity of the family line but also the rights of inheritance to family landed and other property. The politics surrounding land as a major factor of production is not restricted to Igbo society but other African societies, stirring up nationalist agitations and political uprising (Kenyatta 13). In the narrative, the holdings to the family land precipitate violence between the families of Osai and Umeaku until this rivalry is resolved through the intervention of the Ogunano Ezeala, the cultural organization in Umuga, based on the letter written to it by Ogonna and Nnenna.

As Ogonna, the eldest daughter reminisces, women have been socialized by patriarchal codes and institutions to accept the ideological imperative that land is an exclusive male preserve.

When a woman uses her hard-earned resources to secure landed property, the title does not legitimately belong to her but her husband or the male member of her family. Mama had more than her fair share of provocation, oppression from cruel and envious relations... I remember clearly an incident that took place in the year 1967, few months to the outbreak of the civil war. My uncle, Reuben, visited us in Port City and asked Papa to sell to him the four plots of land we have in Enyimba City. To Uncle Reuben's disappointment, Papa rejected his request. He blamed mama for this... Mama wept, bitterly, violated by his taunts, his cruelty. It was after the incident that my sisters and I realized that women were not expected or permitted to own land in our culture even when they pay for it with their own money. If land is bought with a woman's wealth, the real owner of the land is her husband, if she is married. It is viewed as a misfortune to have a family populated by daughters, without a son. It was a shock from which I did not recover for a long time. (94-95)

This traditional episteme, aggravated by the colonialism and imperialism further, drove women to the peripheries of patriarchal African societies (O'Barr and Firmin-Sellers 189).

The land in question here has been bought by Eaglewoman from the proceeds of her bakery but soon becomes family and communal property such that Uncle Reuben is bent on appropriating it for himself. The dire condition of Eaglewoman and her children concerning land rights and title holding is further aggravated with the death of her husband. The politics of alienation from land is accentuated as family members of her husband evoke Umuga tradition to dispossess her of her legitimate property. As the narrator states,

> … a woman's property belongs to her husband who owns her and everything that she calls her own. Since Osai's death, some of his greedy relatives have become bolder, encroaching on the property, daring Eaglewoman to do her worst. Nkemdirim is a minor and does not a strong voice or presence, yet some nights Eaglewoman lies awake, pondering over the justice of some Umuga customs and traditions. What if she did not even have a son at all? She asks herself. Her mind tells her that she knows better than to ask such a foolish question. (58)

Concomitant with Umuga tradition concerning the patriarchal constitution of family property, and especially land as a phallocentric possession, is the traditional imperative of improvising the heir to the family particularly when a male child does not arrive in the family or dies, leaving only female children. This is an Igbo traditional custom which Ifi Amadiume designates as "male daughters, female husbands" (title). Embedded within this phallic custom is the construction of male roles for the daughter who assumes the states of a "man", marries wives and becomes a "husband". The children that are born to her become her father's. The male children from this kind of arrangement thus become "children of tradition" and have the right under phallic ideology in Igbo society to carry on the family line. At other times, the daughter herself bears children as an unmarried woman and they are legitimate children of the father. Usually, the daughter who acquires this character of "maleness" and becomes a "female" husband achieves this status through industry, conscientiousness, courage and accumulated wealth which confer on her such an elevated status. This gender inversion is delineated in the novel when the community dreads the loss of Nkemdirim in an auto mishap. In the event of his death, a vacuum would be created and there will be no male child. Pa Joel, a close friend of Osai's refers to this tradition of male daughters, female husband. He advises that Amara, the youngest of the four daughters who is to be married to a white suitor, Nick in a matter of days, remain in her father's house and produce a son to perpetuate the family. He states in consonance with phallocentric tradition and culture:

> Your brother's accident is a shock we have not recovered from. While we pray for him and hope for the best, we must be prepared to accept God's will. I believe that we have to be ready to face whatever situation we find ourselves in with fortitude, maturity and wisdom. There are issues we must consider whether we like it or not … If I remember correctly, the youngest of you is to be given in marriage on the first day of the New Year,

according to our custom, to the white man ... It is because of this marriage ceremony and the traditional wine carrying ritual that goes with it that I decided to talk to you today. (384-5)

Then Pa Joel appropriates the voice of tradition finally and articulates the message poignantly sparing the women the innuendoes:

Believe me, what I have to say pains me as much as it pains you, I have to say it. Just listen and hear me out. I am counseling that the marriage be postponed indefinitely until we know the fate of Nkemdirim. I say this because it is my opinion that if Nkemdirim returns to his ancestors -- God forbid -- then Amara should remain at home to perpetuate your father's name by producing a son or sons to inherit his vast property and wealth in Umuga and other places. I have said it: these are my words. (385)

Although this articulate male voice is vehemently apposed and roundly condemned by the women including Pa Joel's daughter, Adanna, it foregrounds the pervasive cultural practices that constitute women as lacking individual agency and subjectivity and represents them as mere appendages to men (Tsaaior 30). In this male dominated society, women's definition is executed in, and refracted through, a regime of silence in societal discursive engagements, and invisibility on the contours of a male dominated public arena or space. Even though Pa Joel claims that he appreciates the pain and sorrow of the moment and the exigencies attendant on it, his interpretation of the family mood and temperament is defined and dominated by the assumptions and beliefs of a phallic order. The ancestors he alludes to in the emotional opinion are an all male constellation that wove the tradition to ontological existence in the first place and hence the resistance his words are met with by the matriarchal voices.

This reversal of traditional roles at the behest of a patriarchal ideology is not restricted to Pa Joel's masculinist perspective that Amara should remain unmarried and procreate children for her father's lineage. As a convenient phallocentric strategy to ensure continuity, it achieves its purpose through the subtle process of erasure or exclusion through inclusion. The daughter who is strategic to the efficacy of the traditional practice of providing the (male) heir is effaced from the culture as the male child answers the family (father's) name. This is particularly resonant in the circumstances surrounding Nkemdirim's birth. As the authorial voice affords us and as Obioma, the third daughter reminisces, Nkemdirim is the son of Obioma herself born accidentally out of wedlock. He is a child of circumstance who arrives unexpectedly to fill a vacuum in the family. He is, however, readily appropriated by Osai, the grandfather as a legitimate, biological son. This becomes a sacred secret known only to the immediate family. But transcendent to this, Obioma who is the biological mother leases out the prerogative of motherhood of Nkemdirim to Eaglewoman who becomes the real "mother" and not just the grandmother. Nkemdirim then becomes not just the son but the heir. It is this tradition of "surrogate fatherhood" that Amara must fulfil in fidelity to the male constructed cultural practice and ideological imperative.

Authority, Alterity and Representativeness

The narrative universe of *Children of the Eagle* is dominated by female characters whose agency and dynamic subjectivity has been occluded by patriarchy and its hermeneutic practices. These women are apportioned roles that legitimate male ascendancy, idealise phallic ideology and perpetuate tradition. The authority of the male as a transcendental being in the entire order of creation and his putative superiority over the female is most fully expressed through the singular prerogative of naming his environment (Daly 47). This includes the privilege of being the veritable repository or custodian of sacred tradition, custom and the society's canon and repertoire of cultural ideas and mores whose markers are evident in social codes, religious practices and political and cultural institutions. In contradistinction to this asymmetrical patterning and distribution of roles, women are, according to Mary Jacobus, constituted on the side of lack (5). They are without a meaningful public space. They lack a viable voice to contest power and authority with men and institute negotiations and renegotiations of their status with the men folk. But much more fundamentally, they lack the expressiveness that is a powerful ideological weapon to undermine masculine authority, challenge their marginality and silence and rebelliously recreate, transgressively testify, and subversively inscribe them in the very texture of patriarchal society.

Authority in this perspective signifies "the legitimate capacity to implement and enforce rules governing political institutions" and "because authority is considered necessary to the preservation of political society, analyses of authority often have assumed a central role in moral, political and legal" institutions in society (Taylor 23). In Igbo society (and much of patriarchal African societies) women's strategic significance and symbolic relevance has been occluded by male authority and phallic political ideology. This also informs their ideological representations as a peripheral category that exists to serve and preserve phallocentricity and its authoritarian doctrine of male transcendence and authority.

In the novel, Eaglewoman, a woman of character and strength, is a multiple victim of this authority wielded by men in the name of tradition. She is unfortunate to bring only female children into this world. Within the fabric of traditional Umuga society, this is a major liability since she is "barren" simply because she lacks a son. The daughters are children but their very humanity is hyphenated and not fully recognized by tradition. This is why when Obioma drives herself unwittingly into motherhood and Nkemdirim is born, Eaglewoman readily appropriates him not just to avoid the odium of the community and the ignominy of the family but in a fundamental sense, to satisfy the requisite prescriptions of society that she must have a son. In this society dictated by the male principle, the possession of the phallus is a sacred privilege that confess authority dignity and uncommon prerogatives on the individual. In variance, the lack of a phallus is a major disadvantage that is synonymous with subjugation, exploitation, oppression and repression. Alterity defines the female in the societal engineering process where oppositional binaries are erected on contingences sex and gender hierarchies. This is significant because alterity which negotiates and embeds womanhood within the structures of patriarchal societies like Umuga "designates that which is either opposed to, separate from, or controlled within a closed system" fundamentally because "the notion of alterity or otherness holds a prominent place in the thought" of humanity and is expressed through "racism, sexism, and genocide" (Kosky 8-9).

Eaglewoman herself is codified in this uneven and undemocratic pattern. In an interlocutory exchange between her and Amara, the latter accuses her by being hard on them during cooking lessons and other household chores and sparing Nkemdirim of the rigours and tedium of house-keeping.

"You did not drill Nkemdirim in cooking skills?" Amara charges. "Why?"
"You want to know why? You are female, Nkemdirim is male, that is why." ...
Then Amara protests: "Who says a man should not cook? So a man has a mouth to eat food but not the hands to prepare it?"
Frowning, Eaglewoman snaps back, "If you are not happy with the situation, you can go and sprout a penis!"
"Why should I?" Amara cries vehemently.

"Then say no more about it. Allow us to enjoy the delicious breakfast you prepared." (65)

This conversation does not only underscore the social hierarchies entrenched in Umuga and other traditionally phallic societies but also foregrounds the ideological apparatuses and political superstructures that are elaborately willed into existence by patriarchy. In a pivotal sense, it unequivocally underwrites the central and symbolic significance of possessing the phallus in the society as an organ of privilege, authority and full-valued agency and subjectivity. This is what Nkemdirim enjoys as an exclusive preserve while Amara and the other daughters are bereft of. Women thus become secularized, marginal others in the orbit or circumference of society and its dominant discourses and socio-cultural and political institutions (Spivak 24, 28).

Womanhood: From Repression to Expression

As *Children of the Eagle* has sufficiently demonstrated, women have ideologically appropriated the rites of public space to interrogate and revision their silence, invisibility and subordinate status in male dominated society. The power and ideological potency of female language is perhaps best expressed in the four daughters. Educated and courageous, these sisters resolve, through epistolary means, to enlist the power of the word and language and challenge the Ogunano Ezeala, the cultural organisation concerning the justice and legality of dispossessing a family of its landed property simply because it does not have a male member.

104

By the strength of their letter, the land dispute is revisited and amicably resolved through the fresh staking of the boundary markers. This is a major efficacious and powerful deployment of public space which hitherto is viewed as anathema or desecration of tradition.

In another significant backdrop, the daughters' intervention in the impropriety of conferring chieftaincy titles on departed illustrious and venerable patriarchs of Umuga society to the mutual exclusivity of the matriarchs occasions a revision of the tradition and the recognition of deserving women during the year's Obuofo Day. This enlists women into the canon of achievers and enrols them as co-travellers with men in the history of conspiracies and challenges through the continuum of existence. This power is also evidenced in the four sisters' insistence that they have the legitimacy to inherit their father's property, an act that is considered compromising and transgressive of traditional and cultural norms. In fact, Adanna, Pa Joel's daughter floats a non-governmental organisation, NGO, called Gender Equity Watch, GEW which is devoted to correcting gender imbalances and injustices and attitudes in society. The very universe of the novel is dominated by female characters who are articulate, educated, intelligent and forward-working. The four sisters are all educated just like Adanna. They understand appreciably and adequately their fundamental human rights and freedoms and are positioned to enforce them in a world dominated by masculinity and its hegemony. In the narrative, it is the female characters that are visible, rounded and full-ranged. For instance, in the Osai family, the daughters are the ones who are the moving spirit behind the events.

They travel all alone driving in turns to Umuga without a male comparison to demonstrate their courage and strength of character. They speak for the family. In fact, in the authorial octogenesis, Nkemdirim is even a minor and is technically not represented in the decisions and actions they take vicariously.

It is the same power of expression that confers on Nnenne, the academic and university lecturer to write the family history and codify it in a book. In her representation of biographical matter, Nnenna is resolved to pursue a perspective that will not only privilege and positively portray the family but also wield the weapon of words and mobilise its resources to affirmatively and assertively delineate womanhood as against the pejorative, derogatory and tendentious representations of women in African writing.

This ideological position detracts significantly from the gender politics which Florence Stratton observes of African literary critics who "in characterising African literature,... ignored gender as a social and analytic category" (1). Similarly, the delineation of women in this text revisions Eileen Julien's postulate that "the literature of Africa is replete with valiant and noble heroes-warriors, emperors and kings like Chaka, Mwindo, Sundiata, and Silamaka" (22). Female characters in the novel are ascribed similar qualities even as they contend with the prohibitive codes that define and govern their phallocentric society. In the violent and cataclysmic convulsions of the Nigerian civil imbroglio of 1967-70 which falls within the temporal frame of the narrative, women are presented and re-presented as brave, courageous, war-like and valiant, a representation that was hitherto reserved for men in masculinised narratives by men. What this suggests ideologically is that women are revising these stereotypes, prejudices and myths that demean and cast them unrepresentatively as the weaker or delicate sex and without nobility so that "their subordinate status within patriarchal society is symbolically reinforced" (Carter 6).

The involvement of women in the civil war on the Biafran secessionist side, as the novel reveals, was an acknowledgement of their indispensable role in the liberation struggle and the fabrication of nationhood. This is because woman is the mother of the nation, its soul, with what Ali Mazrui calls "her triple custodial role" (5).

Conclusion

Children of the Eagle affords a narrative canvas on which Akachi Adimora-Ezeigbo inscribes the dominant issues of contemporary significance in Nigeria and other male-dominated societies. In the novel, the competing ideologies of patriarchy and matriarchy enact and re-enact their struggles constituting the society as a contact zone where these asymmetrical relations clash. In this epistemological and hermeneutic schemata, male volubility and visibility is a given while female silence and invisibility on the public arenas of society is dutifully enforced. This socio-cultural ethos which patterns society on the paradigms of sexual and gender binarisms is intensely interrogated and subverted by Adimora-Ezeigbo. The novelist revisions a decadent cultural regime, refracts it as anachronistic and at variance with the kinesis of (post)modernity and re-delineates the boundaries between individuals in society This revolutionary consciousness which is consistent with womanist or feminist movements around the world demonstrates sufficiently the new currents that have become a visible literary and critical trajectory in contemporary African literature.

Adimora-Ezeigbo has a compelling tale to tell in this novel and she has executed this through the creation of powerful female characters and the mobilization of a perspective that privileges womanhood. The female characters she weaves into existence demonstrate a remarkable sense of independence, courage, sound judgement, steadfastness and resilience in the face of discriminatory patriarchal practices. Eaglewoman, for instance, contests the oppressive institutional structures constructed by patriarchy by resisting the appropriation of the family land when her husband is dead. She is assisted by her daughters who are also powerful characters determined to effect change in Umuga community through their intervention in the decision making processes that affect them. The daughters call for the creation of a meaningful space for women through the recognition of female ancestors in the annual Obuofo festival which in the past has been an exclusive male preserve. Through this character delineation, the novelist succeeds in calling attention to the need for the inscription of women into the fabrics of the male dominated society.

Although the story of the novel is rounded and well told, there are instances in which this achievement is compromised. For instance, despite the strong and powerful presence of the female characters, they still exist in the shadows of the patriarchal tradition. The fulfilment of the female daughters in life appears to depend essentially on marriage which is assumed to privilege the men as it a male creation and a strategy to dominate women. In this regard, the novelist has not succeeded in offering viable alternatives open to women to assert their agency and subjectivity in a phallic society beyond the institution of marriage. Allied to this is the fact that though Adimora-Ezeigbo has mobilized sociological details and a felicitous linguistic idiom to tell the story, what emerges is a tale without a cohesive plot because of its fragmentariness. As a result the characters in some cases are not fully developed enough to meet the challenges posed by the plot. What ultimately unfolds is a well crafted story without the necessary corresponding action to propel the plot to a desired resolution. The novel is, however, a compelling commentary on and an insightful negotiation of gender relations in a patriarchal society in a manner that decidedly privileges womanhood and inscribes women into its textures.

Chapter 6

Feminist (Re-) Writing

E.N.Ngwang

OLU Obafemi's article entitled "Towards Feminist Aesthetics in Nigerian Drama: The Plays of Tess Onwueme" in *Critical Theory and African Literature Today* leaves puzzling questions about feminism and feminist criticism in literature. It would seem that Obafemi blames the lack and the lagging behind of feminist criticism in Nigeria and Africa on the absence of women's political movements in Nigeria. Such an approach to feminism and feminist criticism tends to equate literary theory and literature with political activism. However, to attempt to discuss feminist aesthetics in a play without analyzing the feminist elements in the same play is, to say the least, confusing, if not misleading. In fact, feminism or the feminist approach to literature calls for more than a verbal assertion or pointing to feminist aesthetics and politics. It calls for the reader/critic to identify, (re)evaluate and to focus on women and women issues in each work. It also calls for further clarification of whether there is a particularly feminine way of looking at, perceiving, and responding to issues. Are women now engaging in and daring to violate subjects that were supposedly tabooed to women? Would a man and woman looking at the same subject/object (e.g. war) respond or react differently to it because they are biologically different?

The obvious answer to these questions is indisputably in the affirmative (Benstock 1987). That is why *Destination Biafra*, the Nigerian civil war novel, could only have been written by a female, whose motherly sensitivity and instincts captured and acted out the portions of omitted history to the Nigerian Civil war. Emecheta's main character Debbie embarks on a mission to Biafra, which turns out to be a mission of unearthing the forgotten heroines of the civil war, heroines who sacrificed more than the men in an attempt to bring or restore sanity into a male dominated society whose greed for power fueled a senseless war. Armed with their basic feminine instincts and human values, the women fought a war, which they neither completely understood nor negotiated, and lost in substance more than the men lost in politics. They were the silent victims whose bodies were violated by the sadistic male chauvinists who unfortunately considered these women collateral damages, dispensable objects.

Buchi Emecheta has recently won critical acclaim for the portrayal of women in her novels, especially her war novel *Destination Biafra*. These critical approaches to Buchi Emecheta's *Destination Biafra* have emphasized Emecheta's concern with "female militancy" or the role of women in battle or revolutionary movements. Pauline A. Uwakweh in her article "Female Choices: The

Militant Option in Buchi Emecheta's *Destination Biafra* and Alice Walker's Meridian" maintains that "the relevance of Emecheta and [Alice] Walker's fiction in contemporary times lies not only in their historical breadth, but more importantly, in the writers' portrayal of heroines with a strong sense of choice, revolutionary and nationalistic ideals." She goes further to assert, and rightly so, that "in *Destination Biafra*, Emecheta represents the missing female voice and the experience in the Nigerian post war tradition (47-50). Furthermore, Lloyd W. Brown in *Women Writers in Black Africa* comments that

> of all the women writers in contemporary African literature Buchi Emecheta of Nigeria has been the most sustained and vigorous voice of direct, feminist protest.... In Emecheta we detect ... an increasing emphasis on the woman's sense of self, as the writer has matured and as that maturity enables her to deal more and more adeptly and convincingly with the subtleties of characterisation and private introspectiveness. (35)

These critics, among others, recognize Emecheta's inclinations towards a re-evaluation of the status and role of women in post modern African society that complements the lopsided picture of the African society often presented by the men.

In this chapter we examine Emecheta's novel as a re-writing of the Nigerian civil war from a feminist perspective. *Destination Biafra* attempts to capture in vivid terms the terror of the devastating civil war which almost tore Nigeria into two countries. On the one hand, there were the Igbo of Eastern Nigeria who felt that the national or federal arrangement and the distribution of the national cake did not favor them since they had suddenly discovered that the oil wells found in their own part of the country contributed immensely to the GNP of Nigeria. Consequently, the Igbo felt that they had more rights to a larger portion of that wealth. On the other hand, there were the Hausa of Northern Nigeria who strongly believed in "One Nigeria" and who saw in the suggested split of the country a fragmentation which they could not accept, especially as they were in position of leadership. However, in the process of survival or the search thereof, the hidden motives and bitterness that had been harbored by all the factions involved come out. Consequently, Emecheta's novel "expresses indignation and bitterness at both the causes of the civil war and the affliction and undue punishment brought upon a good number of Nigerians and Biafrans" (Porter 325). Were we to accept this as the complete picture of the war, one would be satisfied reading Wole Soyinka's, John Pepper Clarke's and Chinua Achebe's war poetry as analyzed by R.N. Egudu in "Modern African Poetry and the African Predicament." But Debbie's mission to the East (which is the title of the novel) turns out to be more than a recording of the observation and experience of the horrors of war; it is in fact, a "true voyage of discovery" (Porter, 322). Like most of the female African novelists (Herndon 160-61), Debbie lives "to tell her story to educate: to represent what had previously been absent from media representation and colonial education" where women were either ignored or simply used as dispensable objects of sex and procreation. Debbie, an Oxford student soon realizes that she has a mission, one in line with what Sarah Ellis promised: "women have a mission aye!, even a political mission of immense importance! Woman is the regulating power of great social machine" (128).

Debbie is equally engaged in an ambiguous act of self-denial and self-creation which is very significant, especially since constructions of the subjects and self-consciousness are for women, especially marginalized women, profoundly different from the individualistic male model of separate and unique self:

> In taking the power of words, of representation, into their own hands, women project into history an identity that is not purely individualistic ... Alienation from the historically imposed image of the self is what motivates the writing, the creation of an alternate self in the autobiographical act. Writing the self shatters the cultural hall of mirrors and breaks the silence imposed by males [and here I would add the colonizer's] speech. (Friedman 40-41)

Debbie's self consciousness engages here on this journey during which she is able to learn more and more and often in painful ways about the different kinds of wars (civil, sex) that are going on among her fellow citizens, the warring factions, and the motivations behind them. Above all, she learns about herself, her relationship to herself and to others. As she travels to Benin with her mother and their driver, she and her driver and other women are raped repeatedly by bandits-cum-political militia posing as "patriotic Nigerians." Her harrowing experiences continue in Sapele as she beholds the havoc wreaked on other women by some soldiers, and she and some other women are subjected to intense tribal hatred. Debbie also experiences first hand what most ordinary unarmed civilians undergo on a routine basis during the war: women (including the old) are stripped naked, beaten, and violated (leading to pregnant women having premature deliveries) while unarmed men are shot for no reason than that they belong to a particular ethnic group. As part of the global cultural biography that tends to inform female writing, Debbie becomes the extension of Buchi Emecheta expressing the story of her selfhood which is inextricably linked to the female sense of community. In fact, Debbie and her women know very well that they are confronted with two sets of people: the culture makers and preservers (the women) and the culture breakers (the men). These are the subtleties that eluded giant poets like Soyinka who went more for the political ramifications of the war than the human toll.

Soyinka, in fact, looks at the war from a more general perspective. In "Idanre" he presents war as a two-sided sword which cuts its owner as well as its enemy. Its central symbol is the god Ogun, the ambivalent god of creation and destruction. His elitist style tends to float above the reader's head, especially when he commends the passing of Christopher Okigbo whose death spared him the experience of seeing "values turned upside down" (Egudu 104-105).On the other hand, Buchi Emecheta presents war in terms of the human cost and the dispossessing of human life. It is therefore obvious that the motherly spirit in Emecheta inevitably pulled her to evaluate war from the point of view of human losses. For is it not true that the mother is the giver of life, and therefore the protector of this life? The suffering of women, the slaughter of unarmed men and children enhanced the enormity of the barbarism of both camps. In fact, most of the women were not only raped (which was most inhumane and barbaric), but the anger of the fighting factions was aimed at the helpless children of these women thereby subjecting them to multiple victimization. In the face of this monstrosity, we find the women standing their grounds and against all odds.

Although the contending leaders Abosi and Momoh asserted that they were fighting for collective survival, the constant allusion to the oil wealth and political power control downplayed the lofty ideas of political survival. In the novel, the latter claim seems to play a preponderant role in the West in the relationship between the warring Yoruba political leaders Chiefs Odumosa and Durosaro. Such internal conflicts, though localized, uncover the deep-seated yearning for political power and the desire of the local people to hang to such powers even when they had lost or given them up. Therefore, the civil war becomes an extension of sorts of the local wars that are fueled by greed and personality conflicts conjured by the male ego in line with what Judith Newton's judgment passed on the male ego:

Male selfishness and lack of feeling ... are identified as a primary cause of problems in class and gender relations. In the public world of man ... there is no union in the great field of action in which he is engaged, but envy, and hatred and opposition, to the close of the day,-- every man's hand against his brother, and each struggling to exalt himself. (Feminist 129)

Newton then juxtaposes this picture with that of women: "The whole lives of women is but one chain of anxieties, to promote the happiness of all the objects of her heart; surely this attribute overmatches the gigantic energies of ambition and courage of man"(129-30). Unfortunately, this "courage of man" put a wedge between the two tribes – Hausa and Igbo where the latter believe that they are more intelligent and politically destined to rule over the Notherners who are portrayed as naive, ignorant, uneducated even when given the political powers. The Igbo articulate the most persuasive argument against the unholy alliance with the ineffective northern leadership by calling for an independent oil rich Biafra; their destination therefore is not Nigeria but Biafra (60). Abosi seems to be reacting both to the "supposed" mental inferiority of the Notherners as much as to the villainy the Igbo suffered in the hands of the latter when Northern military forces captured and forced the Igbo soldiers to eat their excrement (82). On the other hand, the tribal war clearly reveals the unholy alliance between the Hausa North and the non-Hausa South where the former believes that the southern "Kaferi infidels" are unclean and unfit to rule them:

> The Hausas were at first sorry for the demise of [Onyemere] who only a few days previously had almost been successful in consoling them for their loss. Less than forty-eight hours after the announcement, the radicals again started up their cries about a holy war...shouting, "Death to the Kaferi

infidel!" At the Barclays Bank, they hacked humans to death and those who tried to escape were clubbed and battered to death. "Down with Ibo infidels! Down with the enemy!" they screamed, and the bank workers stared horrified. Anybody who did not have the tribal mark on his face was regarded as Ibo. (87)

The same fate awaited the Igbo in the West and South. Debbie again captures this barbarism in the unfortunate episode of the Igbo wife of the pharmacist in Lagos whose husband was hacked to death. The war therefore becomes one of ethnic cleansing and religious crusading, sidelining the original intention of the first military coups plotters who were out to cleanse Nigeria of political corruption. In fact, three years before the Nigerian Civil War (which constitutes the setting and context of Emecheta's novel), Herbert Spiro had remarked prophetically about this unholy alliance that would eventually lead to dire consequences:

> The maintenance of the unity of Nigerian during the transition from colonial administration to independence was no easy matter, and the survival of the Federation of Nigeria as the most populous African political system still appears doubtful to many. The chief threats came from the extreme cultural diversity of the "country" and the related differences in political development, especially between the south and north.... However, there were also counter-indications suggesting that the constitutional compromise might not endure for long. (157- 158)

The country was precariously built on shifting sand and only waiting for a wind to blow it into shreds. Corruption therefore was only a veneer used to cover the deep-seated power hunger and ambitions of the military who envied the positions of the civilian political leaders. In fact, the military leaders engaged in a much more hideous type of corruption and abuse: sexual. Debbie and her female refugees are raped repeatedly as they struggle to reach their ultimate destination, Biafra. The inhuman treatment, raping and torture and women as described in Chapter 16 entitled "Women's War" captures the entire essence and the ultimate picture of the place of women in this war. This chapter is pivotal to the discussion of women in the novel because it balances the complementary pictures of women as martyrs and as victims:

> Very much later, [Debbie] heard the cries of the women from the mission house, the nuns who felt they were doing God's work and that that would give them immunity from the Soldiers. Debbie guessed what was happening and shed some tears for the octagenerian Irish nun..... Even that old Mother Superior did not escape. They did it to her and then killed her... No, they did not kill her, she just bled to death. They killed the young nuns and many others, but they did not kill Mother Francesca.... She just bled to death. They would never rape an old woman, never... she just bled to death. (224)

This graphic description of the bleeding of these raped old women, the violation of their bodies against a backdrop of

Christianity and the supposed sanctuary which churches were supposed to provide for war victims violate our senses of dignity by any stretch of imagination. This is where Debbie's strength lies: in recording the pictures of the true victims who died time and time again. After all, the unarmed men were simply shot (as if subjected to mercy killing) while the women and children were tortured and left to die unattended. In fact, we are told that,

> Debbie recorded all this in her memory, to be transferred when possible to the yellow scraps of paper she dignified with the name of a manuscript ... If she should be killed, the entire story of the women's experience of the war would be lost. A great deal of what was happening was too dangerous to write down so she had to make her brain porous enough to absorb and assismilate, writing down only key words to trigger off her recollections when she finally sat down to put it all into plain words. She must try to live, not just for the women but for the memories of the boys like Ngbochi. (224)

Hence, we see the victims from Debbie's perspective and the role she has to play to tell their story. Consequently, this novel has two main ideological functions: to bring to consciousness women's experience of the war and more importantly, to challenge conventional constructions of nationalism and heroism. Women too were heroes, even unto death. In this light, Debbie's "account of the war is written from a perspective which is diametrically opposed to that of the dominant gender" (Stratton 127). Women too are capable of great heroism and nationalism:

> Again Debbie marveled at the resources of women. She had seen Uzoma Madako with her husband in Benin, seen the way she sat, her head resting passively on a pole that supported one of the sheds at the motor park: Debbie had seen the way she lifted her eyes as if they were so weighty, had heard the way she spoke in a whisper. And now look at the same woman, only a few days after the death of her husband, she had the courage to slap another woman, to tell another woman to stop indulging in self-pity.
> "Your husband has given you two children, this baby and that girl at home with your old mother. Don't you think you have to make sure you live so that you can look after them? Because the men also gave us a name, you forget your father's name, and in the process of letting your husband provide for you, you have become dumb and passive. Go back to being yourself now. If you are too lazy to farm, you may have to sell your body. But what is new about that? Your children have to live. Get up, women, and let us bury the son of another woman." (214)

Uzoma could not have been more militant and vocal about the political significance of women, born out of their characteristic feelings of love and unselfishness. Her actions here resonate with Judith Newton whose article in Feminist Issues in Literary Scholarship clearly alludes to the dichotomy of gender characteristics: "Male selfishness and lack of feeling... are identified as a primary cause of problems in

121

class and gender relations" (126). In their case, Debbie and her companions have been passive to their men more out of the cultural concept of respect for their husbands than a biological weakness that comes with gender. In fact, and in this outburst, Uzoma trades gender values here where the men become dispensable instruments of procreation and the women the veritable forces of survival, sustainability, and stability. The women do not only have to live but they also have to perform the traditional rites of burial which were formerly reserved for men. This indeed is not the voice of rebellion, but the voice of reasoning, the human instinct for survival. Indeed, the women here break traditional paradigms of life built on empathy and maternal care. Uzoma is not the Lady Macbethan woman who calls on the evil spirits to unsex her in Shakespeare's Macbeth (Act I), but she is the strong voice which asserts that what men can do, women too can do, and even better. But, like Virginia Woolf would say, the women need a room of their own, and given that room, what was counted as a weakness becomes remarkable strength. These women constitute the foundation on which each nation is built. The greatest concern now is to heal the country of its bloodshed and ethnic cleansing, which to Debbie is a very frustrating task. Consequently, she bewails the fate of Nigeria and the political leaders, especially the children:

> I thought after the people like Father were killed things would be all right. Now God help us. Innocent children are suffering- many of them have already been deprived of their parents and now I see more bloodshed. [Alan], why can't you be the ambassador of peace? You people

122

started it. Both Abosi and Momoh were your students, why can't you go and talk to Abosi? (109)

To Debbie, her father and his generation represent part of the imperialistic ruling dynasty that was partly responsible for the war, an element which Kumari Jayawardena refers to in her path-breaking Feminism and Nationalism in the Third World as constituting a bulwark against women's emancipation: the desire to carry out internal reforms must go hand in hand with "the dismantling of those pre-capitalist structures, especially ruling dynasties and religious orthodoxies that stood in the way of needed internal reform" (3). Debbie is in every respect the feminist nationalist, equipped with education (Oxford student) and "self-modernization" as clearly delineated by Robert Young in "Women, Gender and Anti-colonialism" (360-82). In fact, Debbie's plea to Alan is irrelevant because Alan and her Father and the belligerent Abosi and Momoh all constitute the male factors against which the women must resist in order to survive. Both Abosi and Momoh have become so obsessed with winning the war that capitulation or compromise would be considered weakness by either side. The two warlords are now engaged in a battle of personal pride, or rather hubris. None of them wants to appear the weaker of the two. In fact, when it comes to pride, people lose their sense of rational thinking. This explains why Debbie fails woefully in her attempt to convince Abosi, who is poised to fight to the finish in a war that is overwhelmingly not in his favor. Hence, Debbie's assessment of the war effort seems a double-edged truth:

I have the feeling that this is going to be the real fight for independence. What we've had up till now was a sham -the Europeans leaving but putting greedy "yesmen" in the government. Now the young men are fighting for our real freedom, and Biafra may hold the key to that freedom. (114)

Unfortunately, Debbie is mistaken: in the novel, the death of baby Biafra is prophetic as it signals and forecasts the death (defeat) of Biafra. In fact, greed and freedom cannot be bed-fellows in a country where corruption has become the order of the day. Perhaps, Debbie is symbolically referring to the freedom of women who will be left husbandless after their husbands have been killed in the war. Not long after Debbie's assertion, Barbara, one of Debbie's companions to Biafra, paints a more accurate though grotesque picture of the war situation. She recognizes that the country is not just "at war with herself," it is a war fueled by greed for power and encouraged by expatriates, the hovering birds of prey. She muses, "how long will it remain a civil war, with those foreign vultures hovering ready to pounce on the mess we leave behind? Our natural resources, our oil, will be the end of us. Can't those two men see the forces ... wedging themselves between them to encourage the rift?" (112). Barbara implies here that the women see the real picture of the war: the unnecessary killing, destruction of property, raping of women and children. Indeed, this is not a freedom war; neither are the foreign "friends" friends at all, but those who will take advantage of the situation to implant their political agenda and reap economic gains. The British supply the Nigerians with arms and on the other side, the East supplies Biafra with arms. These friendships are carved out of the greedy and selfish desire to find markets for the surplus arms produced by both the East and the West. So the arm producers fan the war while the corrupt local soldiers-turned-politicans use these arms to propagate and satisfy their personal greed for power and eventual control of the oil wealth. Thus, Barbara regrets this unfortunate situation into which the war has plunged the men:

> Any fool of a woman, perhaps, but not men, least of all army men turned politicians. The women and children who would be killed by bombs and guns would simply be statistics, war casualties. But for the soldier-politicians, the traders in arms, who only think of their personal gain, it would be the chance of a lifetime. And the politicians who started it all can pay their way to Europe or America and wait until it has all blown over. (105)

This explains and validates why in the midst of the war and with corpses littering almost everywhere:

> Many Biafran soldiers made illegal profit from food supplies meant for the refugees in Catholic Centers. Girls who refused to go with them were cornered and raped. Many women, however, were willing victims. They saw life as purposeless, anyway. They decided to enjoy their freedom while they had it, and why not with a strong young soldier who could fill one's belly. (221)

The women are tormented, abused, and raped as if they instigated the war. Thus, we see them as the greatest victims of a senseless war, a war whose original motive of cleaning the society of corruption and ineptitude has been subverted by greed, vengeance, and opportunism. The women are subjected to the ignominy of losing their personal dignity, pride and the sacredness of their bodies. The living are worse off than those who are dead because their daily lives will be a perpetual reminder of what they have lost – their sense of womanhood, their bodies that have been abused, mutilated, and disrespected by dirty soldiers who have no guts to approach the women in times of peace. But to Debbie, the message of liberation is totally different. Such sufferings come with the territory and that is why she must rise out of the ashes of her humiliation to assume her position of leadership. She gives herself as the sacrificial lamb to bring sanity to her people. However, she has to continuously shake off her Oxford image and experiences to be accepted by her companions:

> Now she said nothing. She smiled, wanting to share the irony of it with the other women, but she could not, for she knew they would think her arrogant to bring up such topics when they were not even sure they would live to see the next minute. It was at moments like this that Debbie really felt lonely, surrounded as she was by women. Her education, the imported division of class, still stood in the way. She was trying so hard to shake it off, to belong, but at times like this she knew that achieving complete acceptance was indeed a formidable task. These

women would only accept her if they did not know her real background, so she had to keep silent about her store of past experience. (221)

A few pages later, we find her and Uzoma Mandako disciplining Dorothy for accepting a defeatist posture when Dorothy complains that she cannot take care of her children if her husband is killed:

> Shame on you, woman. Shaaaame! ... What type of Ibo woman are you? Which bush community did you come from? What unlucky woman raised you as a daughter? Since when have men helped us look after children. Have you not old people in your cluster of homesteads, to do their job of bringing up the younger ones? (213)

This is a wake-up call for the women who must now take care of themselves and the loved ones in the absence of their husbands. Secondly, Barbara's chastisement of Dorothy goes further than an isolated case: women all along have been care-takers, a role they have played since eternity and which has consistently been ignored. Daughters were raised first and foremost to be care-takers and it was the job of old people, especially old women who stayed at home with the young to bring "up the younger ones." In fact, the war situation simply brings to the fore what women have been doing and will continue to do, especially in traditional African societies. This is a rekindling of feminist ethics which "focuses on women's power, a power that has been denied in patriarchy" (Tomm 109). To fully understand the enormity of this responsibility, we must adhere to Cabral's advice as quoted in Young: focus on the internal dynamics of African societies which lays blame of the continuous devaluation of women in modern African states on capitalism (283-92). Capitalism indeed destroyed the specificity of African cultures by bringing monetary production as a measurement of worth, to a society where women's domestic chores could not be quantified or qualified as economic contribution.

Debbie's rejection of Alan's offer of marriage at the end of the novel goes more with her attempt to continue her mission of self-discovery and rejection of pity than anything else. Were Debbie to accept Alan's proposal at this point, she would have validated the stereotypical and male chauvinistic misconception that women are only good for marriage. Furthermore, the children of the rich are shipped out of the country and the wives of the corrupt politicians use the food crisis in this war situation to enrich themselves. Even at the perils of their own lives, Mrs Ogedemgbe and Mrs Eze (both wives of politicians) organize a clandestine business to sell food at exorbitant prices using Biafran soldiers (214 - 216). We realize here that the children of those who had instigated the war are safely taken away to Europe and the wives engaged in lucrative business, while the poor and the helpless die in their stead. The poor are therefore the victims. In revealing this side of the war story, Emecheta places the responsibility of the Nigerian civil war more on the shoulders of the Nigerians themselves, especially the selfish and egocentric men. And in spite of her sufferings, Debbie assumes the image of the beautiful, black women folk, their warmth, the long suffering victims -the true symbol of Negritude and fortitude.

Destination Biafra brings to mind Bernard M.W. Knox and William G. Thalmann's comments about violence in Homer's The Iliad where the problem of violence and order is presented as both a political as an individual problem. To Abosi, the Biafrans are so deep in war that going back is as difficult as going ahead, and like Shakespeare's *Macbeth*, he would rather go ahead. Violence here cannot be controlled, if not eliminated; neither can it be channeled into safe, creative forms. In fact, violence simply breeds more violence. Though written over two thousand years after Homer's The Iliad and the Odyssey, *Destination Biafra* still addresses the fundamental issues of unnecessary violence and destruction. Consequently, Knox and Thalmann's rhetorical questions about the Greek wars are still as relevant to Emecheta's novel as they were to the Greeks:

How can human aggression be controlled if not eliminated? Can violence within the community be channeled into safe, perhaps even socially creative forms? Can it be successfully controlled by being turned outward, against other communities? If so, does that justify human sufferings and waste that external wars cause? And what about the more refined forms of violence at the heart of social hierarchies that create asymmetries of gender and class? Such are the issues raised by the epics [The Iliad and The Odyssey] amid the formation of the polis, through a long process, to the modern state. Thousands of years later, we cannot claim to have solved them. (118)

Though this assessment of war and violence was in reference to the Homeric epics, it is still a very pointed and vivid assessment of the Nigerian situation where the violence was instead turned inward. It was a situation of dog-eat-dog as the helpless natives, especially the defenseless children and women, were massacred and their bodies violated in a war they never initiated or provoked. The quarrel between the two prominent politicians Chief Oluremi Odusomu and Chief Durosaro over political leadership leads to unnecessary deaths. Friendship is sacrificed on the altar of greed for power, whether real or illusory. Abioseh Porter asserts accurately that Emecheta's depiction of the situation leaves no doubt in our minds that the childish and egocentric actions of the two chiefs contributed directly to the initial wave of killings in the Western region (317):

> At home, the Ogedembes switched on the television, and it was then that they heard what at the time sounded comical and childish, as the squabbles of the two Western chiefs were reported. But then the horrific news started to come. Over thirty people had been killed...thugs had been employed by both sides and innocent people were being killed in the streets... Many market places had been emptied as rival thugs looked for their opponents.
> "Honestly, could not chief Odusomu have given in gracefully? Whose fault was it that he didn't become minister in the Federal House? And after all, five years isn't forever! Stella Ogedemgbe spat in anger.

"That's politics, my dear. I only hope our Prime Minister acts in time to stop more atrocities..."
"Power, just greed for power," his wife started again, her anger mounting. (48-49)

From the above, we may conclude that the primary objective of ridding Nigeria of corrupt and inefficient political leaders was torpedoed by individuals who transformed the national conflict to a conflict of male personalities, the chiefs both males. We also note the breakdown of the nation into camps where political leaders set one camp against another, resulting in the senseless deaths of innocent people killed on the basis of camp affiliation. Personal agendas and pride take precedence over national concerns. The same tug-of-war exists between the two main military leaders-turned politicians. Debbie characterizes the situation in this light:

> It is not a war between Abosi and Momoth. This is our war. It is the people's war. Our very first war of freedom. Momoth and Abosi started the purge, to wash the country of corruption and exploitation. Now there is the danger of the two men putting their self-interest foremost. If that is the case, the war will be taken out of their control and put into the hands of responsible leaders who will see the purge through and restore to us a new clean Nigeria. That is why I am going to Abosi, to warn him not to let himself be carried away by personal ambition to such a degree that he forgets his original aim. (153)

The war has clearly become a contest between Abosi who is out to lead Biafra secede from Nigeria and Momoth who has vowed "to keep Nigerian One" with Debbie as a messenger of peace. Unfortunately, it took Debbie, our heroine, 153 pages, thousands of dead souls, orphans, and women that are raped (Debbie herself included) to come to this realization. Even if the contending leaders realize that the original aim of the war has been subverted, they are so steeped in blood and fighting that retreating is as difficult as going ahead and bear-like (like Macbeth) they will fight the course. They find themselves in exactly the same predicament as Macbeth whose hubris cannot allow him to retreat in the face of imminent defeat. Consequently, Debbie's mission of peace and reconciliation is one of futility, a romance in utopia. However, it is only Debbie, the mother, the female-goddess of sorts who can embark on such a dangerous and selfless mission. To the men, the war is no longer an altruistic desire to reform society, but a show of strength. In this respect, Mamoth and Aboseh look at Debbie as a biological essence, saddled with home and domesticity (Sudarkasa 25). They now look for ethnic groups that are identified by tribal markings irrespective of their political leanings rather than those who oppose their political ideology of unity or secession. As Debbie and the other women continue on their journey of discovery and pain (Porter 324), they learn that the real and perhaps the only victims/sufferers in this war are the most vulnerable people in scociety -the children of the poor and the women. The sons of the rich and the foreigners who profit more from the war are shipped out to Europe, "leaving the Nigerians to go on killing each other if they so desire" (259). Alan Grey's sarcastic remark here truly reveals the carnage that took place, and also how the Nigerians had nobody but their selfish leaders to blame for this war. However, Alan Grey ignored that fact the war was initially fueled by the British desire to impose an unpopular, weak, and unnecessarily proud Northerner, Malam Guru on the rest of Nigeria as Prime Minister when in fact the election process had not ended. They, indeed, sowed the seeds of discontent and the bloody civil war that was to follow, since it turned out that the Prime Minister had no real powers and could not handle the initial crisis between the Igbo and the Hausa (53 - 56). Had the British, the colonial masters, stayed out of the election process, the blood bath that emanated from this election could have been abated. The rightful person, the true choice of the people would have taken over the mantle of leadership. Furthermore, it is Britain through Alan Grey who arranged arms as well as recruited white and black mercenaries from England for the Nigerian military (191); they also ferry the so-called humanitarian relief to Biafra at war with Nigeria. It is this model of external interference that Irving L. Markovitz (1977) and John Cartwright (1984) identify as the deep-rooted problems which destabilized many of post-colonial African countries.

The end of the novel is like the waking from a bad dream. The war of freedom has turned out to be a war of genocide, and the Biafran utopia has evaporated like morning dew with the rising of the sun. As Su Fang Ng argues, the utopian impulses of the Biafrans also fanned the war and the unnecessary genocide. According to Fang

Ng, "in *Destination Biafra*, the utopic longing for the post-colonial nation is unachievable at the present time, but it is only with such ideals that true decolonization can happen" (277). If we go with Fang Ng's evalaution, the unachievable is absurd, useless. The real outcomes overwhelmed the original speculations about the duration of the war and the extent of loss and damage of life and property. The desire of the Igbo to create a nation of their own, free from domination by other ethnic groups, corruption, and exploitation was in itself a utopia, especially as the land contains oil, the very seed of destruction and the major source of export and income for the entire country. This natural gift was finally to be a curse on Biafra on the one hand and on all of Nigeria on the other hand as both belligerent parties laid claim to it.

That is why Debbie's perception of Biafra as an ideal nation becomes misleading, and she confesses, "Biafra seems rather symbolic to me. The ideal that we should all aim to achieve: a nation that has been detribalized, a nation where wealth will be equally distributed" (122). In fact, Debbie sees the future of Nigeria symbolized in Biafra; that is the fraction as a representation of the whole, which the Northerners and Westerners could not fathom. It is this diehard attitude that infuriated Mamoth to say "To Keep Nigerian one is a task that must be done" (141); indeed, Momoth saw the Igbo symbolically as Nigeria's "mosquitoes" (147) which had to be got rid of through the most bloody military operation code-named "Operation Mosquito" (Chapter 11). This use of brute force confirms and reflects what Edmond Keller diagnosed as part of the failure of politics and the use of power in Africa. Keller maintains that "the 1991 African

Leadership Forum, the OAU, made it clear that the denial of democratic rights, and the emphasis of African governments on oppression and militarization, greatly contributed to insecurity in Africa and that the military insecurity, then had a ripple effect, causing insecurity in the social areas " (170-71). The heavy handedness of Abosi and Momoh transformed Nigeria into a military state which, instead of guaranteeing more security, led to tyranny and the tremendous loss of lives. And this insecurity was to continue to envelope the lives of many Nigerians and those of other African states that share borders with Biafra or/and Nigeria. In fact, Abosi fled from Nigeria without resolving the problems his actions had unleashed on the innocent women and children. So no peace talks or truce was brokered between the two fighting factions, and the winner, who in this case was Momoh, was going to take it all.

Throughout the entire novel, Debbie and the other women do not tend to judge the moral issues involved in the war; that is the domain of the men. Debbie indeed emerges as an embodiment of the modern woman, who through personal choice pursues an activity that is proper and sufficient in itself. Her actions are declarations of independence by the black female writer in pursuit of a vocabulary that leads away from the limited rhetoric of powerless virtue and sentimental pathos ascribed to her by male writers and critics. Through and in Debbie, Emecheta demands that we lay to rest the several manifestations of women as objects, mothers, and house keepers. The African woman, the black woman is now the intellectual spokesperson for her own cultural apprenticeship, looking forward to victory. At the end of the novel, Debbie emerges very much like Earnest Hemingway's "old man" Santiago in The Old Man and the Sea who confessed that a man may be destroyed but not defeated. There is indeed a certain degree of grace even in her traumatic rape experiences, near-death escapades, and starvation.

As the novel ends, there are echoes of the voices of the dying, the young who had not lived to tell their stories, the women who are emitting the pains of their violated bodies and bruised womanhood. Debbie is very sensitive to these cries because the children are an extension of the female principle. Her greatest pain is that she is helpless mother-figure who, unlike the sweet mother in Prince Nico Mbarga's famous song "Sweet Mother" (2007), cannot give solace to the ailing child. However, she is the voice petitioning for intervention and humanitarian assistance that defines her maternal qualities. She and those voices resist to be eclipsed by the thundering voices of the bombs and the men. Debbie, the victim-narrator says it all very pathetically: "They [the children] were orphans, like hundreds of other children who were victims of the decisions made by adults [men] of whom they had never heard and would never see..." (210).

Chapter 7

Twice-Betrayed People

M.De La Cruz-Guzmán

YVONNE Vera designs her last novel *The Stone Virgins* (2002) as a counter-narrative to her overtly pro-nationalist novel *Nehanda* (1993). In doing so, she highlights the relevance of trauma theory and the decline of postcolonial Zimbabwean nationalism to her novels which opens narrative space for formerly marginalized voices from the liberation struggle and exposes the lies ingrained in the nationalist meta-narrative that these novels strive to counter. Thus, trauma theory and the concept of witness or testimonio literature will be used to explore the paradigm of double traumatization of the character Sibaso and its consequences for Zimbabwean civil society, and these will authenticate and provide clinical support for Vera's representation of trauma in both *Nehanda* and *The Stone Virgins*.

The theoretical paradigm of double traumatization in relation to postcolonial texts allows this article to open a new space for the analysis of previously marginalized voices that are now being acknowledged and validated in the process of clarifying that their experiences stem from two separate but intertwined assaults on their existence. It is here asserted that the indigenous Zimbabwean populations to whom Vera gives voice in her literary works have experienced a double traumatization that, combined with a post-independence decline in nationalism, fosters an environment in which peoples who were first assaulted by European colonial forces suffer a second even more difficult betrayal trauma from the most unexpected source: fellow indigenous people working under the banner of Zimbabwean Nationalism.

While the first betrayal strengthened the people's reliance on one another both as members of the oppressed community and as potential partners in the fight for independence, the second betrayal seems to alienate and to obliterate their basic belief in and practice of hunhu. This psychic shift is an additional detrimental side effect of the assaults which is particularly relevant in an analysis of the character of Sibaso, arguably the least logical choice in the novel of an author who strives to provide a voice for marginalized women, but it is this very illogicality that renders this study able to draw a more thorough analysis of the double traumatization experienced by all the testimonio-providing characters.

To analyze the components of double traumatization and the interconnectedness of these two traumas, it is necessary to first survey the field of trauma theory and then make clear the departures and new contributions of the double traumatization theoretical framework. Post-Traumatic Stress Disorder (PTSD) was officially included under its current name in the Diagnostic and Statistical Manual of Mental Disorders (DSM-III) published in 1980, and this inclusion along with its fourteen years of subsequent revisions and updates to create DSM-IV, published in 1994, have legitimated the diagnosis of this mental health disorder and have, even more importantly for this project, expanded its diagnosis beyond war-ravaged individuals. In fact, The Journal of Traumatic Stress and PTSD Research Quarterly were both created to provide a new space in which to consider broader PTSD research.

In its post-DSM-IV form, PTSD's definition has been expanded so that the qualifying trauma is no longer only war related but can emerge from any "trauma inducing experiences such as rape, abuse, disasters, accidents, and torture" (Beal 918). This expanded definition which still requires a traumatic trigger for the series of symptoms, has given way to a new critical trend in literature often termed Trauma Theory and most often identified with Cathy Caruth's work. While Caruth still relies heavily on a Freudian cosmology for her treatment of trauma in narratives and narrative trauma, she has opened an important space for scholars to build on trauma theory and create new theoretical paradigms for postcolonial studies.

Lenore Terr's definition of trauma is most appropriate for the literary texts at hand: "Psychic trauma occurs when a sudden, unexpected, overwhelming intense emotional blow or a series of blows assaults the person from outside" (8). Judith Herman further posits that it is an assault that causes fear and terror. Thus, for the purpose of this study, literatures of trauma are those that deal with overwhelming assaults from outside or their aftermath of fear and terror. Often these literatures focus on war and its effects on the human psyche. Standing on the shoulders of western giants such as Freud and Janet, however, is a dangerous proposition for the postcolonial scholar who must step away to change the symbolic representations to reflect appropriate indigenous or creole cosmologies and key figures for symbolic representation of the "abnormal traumas [war, genocide, political violence, untimely death]" which Caruth grounds in Freudian terms (13). Thus, the key figures in this analysis and Vera's novels are particularly Shona culture specific and not necessarily Oedipal.

The assertion that postcolonial peoples are recovering from a double traumatization in this paper is a unique contribution to the field of trauma studies, which has been mostly associated with the study of the Holocaust and the Vietnam War and has thus limited its application to other global events such as the original German holocaust perpetrated against the Herero people of Namibia and the massacres of indigenous peoples in Matabeleland, Zimbabwe. This new critical framing of trauma allows a unique approach to inform the novels of Vera as testimonio literature and to deconstruct the multiple traumas inflicted upon the main characters that provide their counter-narratives to previously accepted history.

In this conception of double traumatization in a postcolonial and post-nationalist environment, the culturally specific concept of hunhu in Shona society is privileged in the framing and renegotiation of the Freudian concept of traumatic repetition so that it is applicable and pertinent to this culturally specific analysis of a Sub-Saharan narrative. In this forum we must intentionally reject the hegemonic application of western critical thinking in favor of more culturally-driven theoretical frameworks that engage the literary texts in more relevant and critically useful ways that privilege the indigenous authors, cultures, and histories and open spaces for formerly marginalized voices in the postcolonial world.

In a postcolonial setting, there is always an original trauma that causes PTSD: colonial rule. Thus, colonization imprints a first traumatic assault on the minds of the previously subjugated indigenous peoples. As a coping mechanism, however, individuals cling to their communities and their sense of interdependence with other human beings to reaffirm their own humanity and to stand against the hegemonic powers that choose to devalue their humanity. This first betrayal strengthens the people's reliance on one another both as members of the oppressed community and as potential partners in the fight for survival and independence. However, the PTSD is evident in their daily lives as intrusive memories and flashbacks, emotional numbing, avoidance, and an exaggerated startled response to stimuli which betrays the individual's mental health disorder. Added further is the claim of "double traumatization" defined here as two distinct yet incremental sets of experiences that cause fear and terror and are outside the normal range of human experience which when combined produce a damaged psyche.

The second trauma is categorized as betrayal trauma which is unique because "the people or institutions we depend on for survival violate us" and "the core issue is betrayal -a betrayal of trust that produces conflict between external reality and a necessary system of social dependence" (Freyd 1). In this narrative context, avoidance, amnesia, and pathological dissociative responses that help the individual to keep threatening information from awareness are triggered by the betrayal. Furthermore, there is a loss of volume control and traumatic reenactment which compels the victim to repeat the action without knowing that he or she is repeating it because it is his or her way of remembering. Thus, the double traumatization model developed here implicitly includes colonialism as the first trauma factor and betrayal trauma as the second factor, and in doing so, complicates the normal treatment of literature through the critical lens of trauma theory.

In this context of double traumatization, Yvonne Vera's novels *Nehanda* and *The Stone Virgins* serve as catharsis for the Zimbabwean people who suffered the first trauma of a colonial invasion and its subsequent oppression, as catalogued in *Nehanda*, and a second betrayal trauma delivered by the Nationalist's deadly military forces in the immediately post-independence period, as narrativized in *The Stone Virgins*. As an indigenous woman, Vera is a direct descendant of the originally traumatized and a contemporary and close neighbor, as a resident of Bulawayo, of those who were betrayed by the nationalist massacre of the 1980s. Thus, it could be argued that she is part of the collectively traumatized indigenous people of Zimbabwe and is thus uniquely poised to write this narrative. In other words, she provides the words Nonceba strives to find at the end of the novel.

By accepting, to a limited extent, Caruth's claim that literature should be reread as an extension of Freudian studies of trauma (3), but privileging Fanon's concept of a Black man's "neurotic condition," a psychoanalytic approach to the study of Vera's novels and their characters, but with a non-western set of "key figures" for symbolic representation of the war, genocide, political violence and untimely death, is hereby employed. Thus the key figures in this text are particularly culture-specific instead of Oedipal. Bones, spirit mediums, Nehanda, Kaguvi, spiders, trees, seeds, and aunts resonate within the Zimbabwean and African symbolic discourse. Consequently, the different expressions of post-traumatic stress syndrome are acculturated to this sub-Saharan setting as well.

In this narrative context, avoidance, amnesia, and pathological dissociative responses that help the individual to keep threatening information from awareness are triggered by the betrayal by "creating a disruption in the usually integrated functions of consciousness, memory, identity, or perception of the environment" (Bloom 7).

In the case of the dissident and the Fifth Brigade members, there is a loss of volume control, also known as a distorted internal system of arousal, and a repetition compulsion that becomes the victim's way of remembering. The combination of the latter change Sibaso and the Fifth Brigade soldiers from victims to victimizers as they become addicted to trauma as a soothing and stimulating mechanism (Bloom 9), so they remove themselves from the role of victim and assume the power of those who terrorize and abuse others. Thus, this double traumatization and inability to heal themselves lead them to the most disturbing outcome: a state of being both "a fragile spider" that fears being easily erased and a "hungry, predatory spider" that inflicts further trauma on others.

This disjuncture is at the crux of Vera's narrative for it truly opens spaces for the most marginalized of voices, and it authenticates the counter-narratives of all the survivors, including the most horrific and problematic figures, such as Sibaso the dissident and the Fifth Brigade. The perspective insists on acknowledging colonial hegemony and violence, yet also reiterates the double culpability of these brutally oppressive European systems in modeling and creating a new indigenous people who moved from victim to victimizer under the auspices of nationalist ideologies that betrayed and marginalized the very people they were supposed to unite. Thus, postcolonial literatures and counter-narratives are in a unique position to decentralize Western epistemology and produce a counter-memory that contradicts the perpetrators' grand narrative and opens critical spaces for the retelling of a more inclusive indigenous narrative. That space is used to explore the brutal actions of the dissident and the Fifth Brigade soldiers because Vera positions them as victims-turned-victimizers who were, themselves, defrauded in the post-independence period. Therefore, they, like their victims, are uniquely poised to provide insights into the mind of a Zimbabwean character that has experienced betrayal trauma.

The first trauma to the indigenous people of Zimbabwe, formerly known as Southern Rhodesia and then Rhodesia, was the imperialist racism imposed upon the people with the 1890 British invasion which resulted in what psychiatrist Hussein Abdilahi Bulhan categorized as

> the generalization, institutionalization, and assignment of values to real or imaginary differences between people in order to justify a state of privilege, aggression, and/or violence. Involving more than the cognitive or affective content of prejudice, racism is expressed behaviorally, institutionally, and culturally.(13)

Thus, in Southern Rhodesia, the indigenous Shona and Ndebele peoples were assigned sub-human value whose only purpose was to abandon their own culturally rich traditional ways and strive, instead, to be good Christian, English-speaking laborers and servants to the colonists and missionaries. Thus, a British official in Nehanda pledges to retrain them to leave behind their own self-government and their normal agricultural pursuits so that he can "teach them the most gainful use of their time" so that it can be "invested in labour" that will benefit the English crown (55).

Frantz Fanon appropriately argued that since the indigenous person "lives in a society that makes his inferiority complex possible, in a society that derives its stability from the perpetuation of this complex, in a society that proclaims the superiority of one race; to the identical degree to which that society creates difficulties for him, he will find himself thrust into a neurotic situation" (100). This original assault on the indigenous person's dignity and humanity leaves him or her traumatized and with limited possibilities of recovery since rebellion is suppressed and submission demanded. All the same, in 1896, the Zimbabwean people took arms in the first chimurenga, or liberations struggle, because the "neurotic situation" was simply unbearable, and the people, especially in remote rural areas, still had clear connections to their ancestors and traditional ways, including the outright leadership of the Shona mhondoro Nehanda, a royal ancestor spirit. As described in Vera's pro-nationalist novel *Nehanda*, despite their defeat, the people were able to create a rich oral history because "hope for the nation is born out of the intensity of newly created memory," and this memory centered around the figure of *Nehanda*. It was based on her leadership, "her refusal to accept conversion to Christianity, her defiance on the scaffold, and her utterance of the famous prophecy: "'my bones will rise' to win back freedom from the Europeans" (Lan 6). Thus, a national hero was born for the indigenous people, and faith in her words would shape a nationalist spirit among the people of Zimbabwe and guide the freedom fighters to independence nearly a century later.

The first rebellion was suppressed, however, and the people would have to wait until the 1970s to attempt another and successfully bring independence to Zimbabwe. Thus, the intervening years had their traumatic effects on a defeated people who were all the more oppressed by colonial land redistribution that deprived them of their own fertile lands and confined them to arid communal lands. In *Nehanda*, the narrator points out the greed of the newly arrived British as she describes the Shona's willingness to show the British where to find gold and the latter's reluctance to leave once it was found because "now they hunt us out of our land. Is it not clear that they have discovered that our land is the gold they sought?" (66). As Bulhan posits, even today, "the world is still reeling from the historical avarice and violence Europe unleashed upon it...Europe's greed to own and control has had a profound impact on human history and psyches" (36). Vera's Nehanda successfully lays the groundwork for an understanding of a nationalist myth while also showcasing the reaction to British avarice and indigenous dehumanization and displacement in the country. The combined trauma from colonization and colonial suppression of rebellion is thus clearly visible even today in Zimbabwe. Despite having earned liberation in 1980, the economic realities of the indigenous peoples did not change substantially after independence.

The second assault of the postcolonial indigenous peoples of Zimbabwe was the betrayal trauma inflicted by the very nationalist forces that were supposed to unite the people under majority rule, bring a more equitable distribution of resources to the dispossessed, and restore dignity to the majority of people and their traditional customs. The attack on their human dignity was unexpected because the attackers were fellow indigenous people who, "overcome by a consuming desire for ownership and self-aggrandizement" (Bulhan 36), a clear colonial legacy that disrupted their previous communal societal infrastructure, betrayed their supporters and their very own people's dreams of equality and access. In the Zimbabwean case, the betrayal trauma, the key second assault in the double traumatization model, came in the form of the immediately post-independence massacres in

Matabeleland, as reported in *Breaking the Silence, Building True Peace. A Report on the Disturbances in Matabele! land and the Midlands, 1980-1988.*

It was this unwarranted use of force on the government's part against the average Ndebele civilian that led to the abuses catalogued by the CCJP's report that was made public in April of 1999, over a decade and a half since the beginning of the massacre. It is this particular reality of government-sponsored terrorism against its citizens during early independence, which showcased the internal division in Zimbabwe and the overall decline in nationalism carefully hidden from the population, that inspired in Yvonne Vera such an outrage she decided to take back all the support she had given nationalism in writing Nehanda – although it still stands as witness to the original trauma of the Zimbabwean people under colonial repression – and to expose in The Stone Virgins the horrors of a twice traumatized people who were betrayed after independence by the very trusted nationalists who were supposed to unite them in the quest for a more egalitarian Zimbabwe.

The group of ex-combatants, both male and female, who emerge from the second chimurenga still intoxicated by the dream of freedom but quickly realize that the nationalist rhetoric which once spurred them on in battle is now empty and solely based on political expediency merit a careful textual analysis in light of this second traumatization, namely betrayal. The first group that Vera so clearly outlines in The Stone Virgins is that of the male war veterans who technically "returned form the war with all their senses intact except for that far away traveled look that makes the girls a bit fearful" (47). They are first mentioned as guarding their loneliness even as the Kezi women worship them for leading them to independence, but this worship is based on the nationalist propaganda they have heard and internalized during the long war. Thus, Vera forces the Kezi women to acknowledge that the men "who walk awkward like, lost like, as though the earth is shaking under their feet, not at all like what they imagine heroes to be" and are unable to look a woman in the eye for long are, in fact, damaged by the war (48). Once they discover the nightmares of the men, their inability to truly connect with others, namely disassociation, and their unwillingness to share the truths and realities of combat, they realize that these men are not the same men who left the village. The post-traumatic stress syndrome, especially these intrusive symptoms of nightmares and flashbacks, that the average ex-combatant is suffering is not addressed by the government, and the men are not given any resources to cope

The most that these men can do is express their outrage against being judged by nationalist rhetoric and its unrealistic standards as they assert forcefully that they have not killed anyone, especially not a white man, and urge their listeners to understand, "that is all talk because the country needs heroes, and flags, and festivities, and the notion of sacrifice" (48). They are aware of the realities of combat, survival in the bush, and the daily activities of war that left them physical and emotional wounds which they are unable to heal. Hence, Vera says of one ex-combatant, "his tone is pleading for her to stop examining his wounds and hindering his view of the hills" (48); the latter phrase is particularly significant as it points to his reliving the past by looking at the hills that represent so much of the struggle for Zimbabwean veterans. As war vets, they are at least more superficially concerned with reinserting into civil society, which has not changed as promised by the nationalist rhetoric, than they are with the hero status that their fellow villagers want to accord them. They balk at the question of whether they killed a white man and focus instead on the quotidian, such as finding a spouse and a place in their village again, as long as it doesn't interfere with their connection to the memories of war.

The nationalist myth of equality, spiritual leadership, and improved livelihoods falls short in reality for these men. They are outraged by the non-combatant's willingness to believe in the myth that they now know is not actually true. In addition, they return to lives that are substantially similar to those they left behind, so they know that the improvements promised by the struggle for liberation are more theoretical than actual. They are clearly disappointed by their new realities and fail to truly be present in their new relationships and positions in life. Instead, the ex-combatants focus, consciously or not, on the wartime experiences they had during waking hours with their gaze always on the hills and during sleeping hours with nightmares, "flailing arms," and "voice darker than night"(49), and they appear to disassociate from the very quotidian life they seek to reestablish.

The attitudes of the male veterans toward nationalism are justified by their experiences and are the beginning of a strong decline in nationalism, but the female veterans' experiences prove the betrayal of their hopes and dreams is even more painful than that of their male counterparts for it places them as women back in subservient roles that nationalism had proclaimed obsolete for its ex-combatants. Vera first introduces these veterans in the following passage:

> the women who return from the bush arrive with a superior claim of their own. They define the world differently. They are fighters, simply who pulled down every barrier and entered the bush, yes, like men. But then they were women and said so, and spoke so, and entered the bush, like men. To fight like men, and said so, to fight, like women who fight. (49)

Namely, the women have taught the country that women fight and that they are still women, not "like men" but deserving of their own place of privilege in the struggle for independence for which they risk their lives. The excerpt implies redefinition of a worldview, for according to Rudo Gaidzanwa, "the strong women [in Zimbabwean life and literature] are prostitutes, gangsters, and disobedient wives or daughters" (97). Thus, Vera's *The Stone Virgins* expands this power to female ex-combatants who stand against traditional societal rules but are at least temporarily immune to its censorship because of their role in the liberation struggle. They set an extra item on the agenda for post-independence Zimbabwe, for they overtly call for gender equality and recognition in an African context of honoring ex-combatants and acknowledging and privileging their experience and knowledge in the struggle.

In setting new expectations for women's independence, these freedom fighters awaiting the announcement of independence during the ceasefire set their own societal norms that are often contrary to the more male-privileged standards of traditional Shona and Ndebele society. Vera illustrates these changed behaviors in their everyday interactions, for "they do not apologise for their courage and long absence nor hide or turn away from the footpath" (50); instead, they assert their presence and their right to stay on the path and to be seen wherever they go, including Thandabantu. In their war vestments, they " pull out cigarettes and smoke while standing under the marula tree...and walk leisurely to Thandabantu Store; slowly as though they have a lifetime to consider what independence is all about" (51). The passage is significant because their clothing signals that these women are not bound to homes where they must keep their home, prepare meals, tend to the fields, raise children, and care for spouses or parents. Thus, the independence from these obligations is worth noting for them as they honestly consider what other kinds of freedoms might come to them now that the struggle is over.

They also listen to soccer matches on the radio with the men although they do not choose to engage in conversation with non-combatants. Thus, they enjoy the privilege of full participation in what are normally male activities, as well as a more egalitarian sense of being because even their breasts, a traditional and essentialist focus of femininity, are

> held carelessly up as though they are nothing but another part of the body where some human life just might be nurtured and survive, the breasts only a

shape on the body, like the curve of the shoulder, a useful but wholly unremarkable part of the anatomy. (Vera 52)

These women can then exist without the societal norms and limits imposed upon their gender, and this is the expectation that they have for life in post-independence Zimbabwe.

As another sign of post-traumatic stress, the women wear camouflage because it is the only way to keep the privileges they have grown accustomed to having during the war. Civilian clothing would sexualize them and render them powerless once again in their communal societies, but these war time vestments also allow them to stay in the 'struggle mentality' in which they must be cautious, alert to danger at all times, unable to make small talk and form casual relationships, and somewhat disassociated from the community around them. In fact, the men want the experience of war by proxy and wish the women would speak to them about it, but the women will not be used and they will not yet engage, so they do not interact at all beyond being present. Instead, they appear to be "mighty and serene women whom nothing seems to disturb" (54). However, Vera notes that "the female soldiers marked with unknowable places on their own faces, with an unquenchable sorrow around their eyes unaccustomed to a sudden stillness such as this, a sedentary posture and mindset, no longer wanderers, not threatened or threatening, these women hold their peace and say nothing to condemn or negate, but kept their distance a while to gather all the evidence they can about the other's cherished hope" (51). Thus, they still engage in disassociation, an avoidance symptom of post-traumatic stress syndrome, and cannot yet put down the war-time mentality that has been their everyday standard in favor of a re-engagement and reinsertion into civil society, and the use of camouflage and lack of association with non-combatants render them still in the throes of post-traumatic stress, which they are not able to address.

Furthermore, the men clearly state that this time of awe and honoring the female ex-combatants is not long-lasting and that in the near future, they will fade away and so will this debt the men feel toward them. Thus, "they panic, knowing they will never be a time like this again and that next time they see these women they will no longer be these women and no moment at all will continue to exist" (54-55) because once the excitement of independence is over, there will be traditional roles to reestablish and these women will once again become accessible lovers, mothers and aunts. In other words, they will be ordinary and with that change will come the disappointment of the women who are not only experiencing post-traumatic stress syndrome but who also experience a betrayal by the nationalist government that argues their work during the struggle was based on cooking, washing, and minor combat and thus excludes them from positions of power.

While the ex-combatants in the novel provide important counter-narratives for the retelling of history, Vera's main protagonists are civilians. In particular, the sisters Nonceba and Thenjiwe come to embody the abuses and betrayal of the nationalist regime, and Mahlathini illustrates the double traumatization of the indigenous peoples because all three are ordinary citizens who became victims in the massacres that followed independence. An analysis of their betrayal necessitates a concurrent discussion of the perpetrator's betrayal by the nationalists. In addition, these main characters in The Stone Virgins have direct antecedents in Nehanda and can clearly be identified as such in a close reading. This is particularly relevant because the intertextuality is indisputable.

In fact, a close reading of the Fifth Brigade's attack on Mahlathini and the Thandabantu Store reveals the consistent betrayal of civilians and combatants alike. In this case, Mahlathini's store is the social and economic hub of Kezi. The store is the last stop in the Bulawayo-Kezi line, the only source of goods for the community, and the gathering place for watching sunsets during discussions of the day's events, politics, the struggle, and dreams of independence. Mahlathini, himself, is described as a mild mannered man who refuses to make eye contact while doing business at the store because "he does not want to remember who said what, and when. He does not want to know who heard him say what, and when" (120). In other words, he knows that he and his business are at the center of this community, but he refuses to become personally involved in politics so that his store is always open to all who would like to ease onto its famous veranda. He is the typical civilian happy to learn all about the important events in the country but not truly connected in any direct way to them. He lives on the margins of the greater societal changes but at the center of his small community where he can truly enjoy the life of the average Zimbabwean and make a living that truly benefits everyone around him. He is not optimistic or pessimistic about the prospects of independence because he knows that life will not change significantly for him, but he is happy to learn about the details from his customers as they pass through his store.

It is this fascination with current events and life of Kezi that provide him with a direct antecedent in Vera's previous novel Nehanda. The resonance with the earlier novel's young boy who is atop a Musasa tree overlooking his village when he becomes fascinated with the sight of "two people sitting on cows. The boy observes them with increasing interest. He has never seen people sitting on cows" (96) much as Mahlathini has never seen people so thrilled by the prospects of independence. This fascination with the novel and the discovery that the animals are not actually cows is so hypnotic that the boy fails to warn the village that white men are attacking. Likewise, Mahlathini's fascination with the social life of Kezi and its connections to the country on the brink and immediately after independence render him incapable of taking in relevant information about the military forces gathering around Kezi that could have saved his own life and could have warned all of Kezi about the assaults that were to come.

While in the aftermath of the village massacre, the boy wishes to die and the slow healing of his injuries, both physical and emotional, remind one of the concept of resurrection, Mahlathini's actual death points not to hope but to absolute betrayal. The hope provided by the child in Nehanda is that of a new liberation struggle which will come in the future because the spirit of Zimbabweans is not completely smothered by the surprising British victory in the first chimurenga, but in *The Stone Virgins*, the betrayal of Mahlathini and consequently the whole town that depends upon him, as part of the Matabeleland massacres, represents the Nationalists' violent betrayal of the civilian population they were supposed to protect and represent. Mahlathini's death provides no counterpart for hope and resurrection of the Zimbabwean spirit of independence.

Mahlathini's death is characterized by his own very particular reactions to the assault and a very violent series of attacks on him by a clearly established Fifth Brigade. His reactions, as a civilian uninterested in partaking personally of political struggle, are very contained and are similar to those he had when working the store till, so he never looked up at the soldier accusing him or registered any details that would allow him to process who was going to kill him. Vera states, "he had a shocked and lingering fondness for independence; the many soldiers on the porch, their bodies spread like new flags under his roof," (122) and he did not wish to acknowledge that this violent reality was possible in post-independence Zimbabwe since it was precisely this kind of repression that had spurred the fight for freedom. Acknowledging this possibility would have reinscribed the trauma suffered under colonial repression thereby aggravating the assault. Still, the former soldiers shot everyone in his store, including old men and children, and "made a perverse show of his death, accusing him of offering a meeting place where anything could be spoken, planned, and allowed to happen" (121). Ironically, this charge would have been considered quite patriotic during the actual struggle, but in post-independence Zimbabwe split by pro-ZANU and pro-ZAPU forces, this was a crime equally punishable by the Fifth Brigade, the rest of the nationalist military forces in the area, and the dissidents they purported to attack. Mahlathini refused to protest the charges or engage in any way. His denial and disassociation at this point is complete because there is a definite "disruption in the usually integrated functions of consciousness, memory, identity and perception of the environment" (Bloom 7). In a state of deliberate passivity, he submitted to their verdict knowing full well that he would die and unwilling to give up his belief in and fondness for the nationalistic rhetoric that had touched him so profoundly.

The soldiers then tortured him and lit the entire store on fire so that he died in the fire. Vera states, "before they had shaken off the flour from their arms, they had already forgotten Mahlathini and the pillar of flame they had left behind" (123). Such was the training of the Fifth Brigade and the betrayal of both this infamous post-independence military unit and the civilians in the area. The government had chosen not to assist its former soldiers to readjust to society in favor of training them for anti-civilian operations intended to strengthen ZANU's dream of a one-party state. Thus ZANU failed to serve the very soldiers that brought it to victory, and is now out-of-favor with its alliance partner ZAPU because of a misguided desire to destroy the alliance and create a ZANU-led nation. In pursuing this interest, Prime Minister Mugabe authorized a series of military units to be retrained for anti-civilian deployment, and he created the infamous Fifth Brigade to carry out his particular political will without any accountability to the regular military order.

The men who were recruited for these activities were not only victims of post-traumatic stress syndrome but also re-victimized with training that compelled them to repeat and relive the experiences of war without an honorable cause or the well-being of their country's citizens at heart. Thus, these victims are turned into victimizers, and the civilians in Matabeleland and the Midlands are betrayed by the nationalist government that sees them not as citizens and former freedom fighters but as expendable civilians with the potential to harbor former ZAPU freedom fighters who are now labeled 'dissidents' and persecuted by the government. Ironically, the CCJP report confirmed that while there were approximately 200 dissidents who did commit random crimes of violence, which were mostly directed against white commercial farmers, the vast majority of the violations of indigenous human rights were, in fact, committed by governmental military forces (10). Thus, the betrayal trauma was widespread, including even those who carried out the atrocities.

Mahlathini serves as the epitome of the civilian non-combatant because while he is charmed by the nationalist rhetoric, like the men and women of Kezi, he does not directly engage in political struggle or intrigue. He prefers simply to be informed and to enjoy the possibilities of freedom and independence for his people. He welcomes all to his store, and he fails to engage enough in politics to predict the massacres that would befall him and his community. Thus, his trust in a nationalist agenda is absolute, and even when confronted with the betrayal, he chooses denial over acknowledgement of such a personal traumatization. Denial and disassociation are valid responses because the horror of his own death in the context of betrayal would be a considerable shock that would merit such an impairment of his "normal emotional interaction" and require "splitting off experience from our feelings" (Bloom 7). Mahlathini's reaction is similar to that of civilians across the nation who heard rumors of these massacres but chose to believe this impossible in light of a post-independence, majority-rule state.

The second set of civilians is the sisters Thenjiwe and Nonceba. Their characters are particularly important to Vera not only because they represent the betrayal trauma of the civilian population in terms of their personal safety and communal ancestral spirituality but also because their counter-narratives are consistent with Vera's commitment to opening spaces for marginalized women's voices. Their representation of the former becomes clearer when the two characters are analyzed separately and grounded in their counterparts in Vera's earlier novel, Nehanda. In Nehanda, Thenjiwe and Nonceba have antecedents in the two sisters coming from the Matopos hills carrying water on their heads. When they reach their village, they are massacred by the British while their little brother watches from atop a tree (94-5). In addition, Thenjiwe can clearly be connected to the similarly motherless Nehanda who is clearly identified with the imagery of divining bones, hakata, predicting that "a spirit intends to manifest itself in Nehanda" (50) and she is a mhondoro, or lion spirit, so that she is like Kaguvi, her fellow medium, connected with the leg of the lion.

Thenjiwe is used to represent Nehanda and her ancestral spirit since she is closely associated with bones in the later novel. Her lover, Cephas "loves her bones, the harmony of her fingers, he loves most the bone branching along her hip.... This he loves, this bone in her, as it is the deepest part of her, the most prevailing of her being, beyond death, a fossil before dying" (32), thereby providing echoes of Nehanda's prophetic words that her bones would rise again and a direct reference to the leg bone of the lion that renders the mhondoro special ancestral spirits.

In the earlier novel, Nehanda is also poignantly depicted as lifting "her small water gourd carefully to the top of her head, her hands trembling" because when water spills over her shoulders she feels frightened (18). Given Nehanda's ability to go forward and backward in time, this fear is justified in *The Stone Virgins* as the water from Thenjiwe's bucket spills over her body when she is decapitated. Furthermore, in the earlier novel, the mhondoro Nehanda is the landscape and the landscape is written on her body, so the character is stunned when "she looks up in surprise and her body has changed from water to stone" (1). Likewise, Thenjiwe is described by Vera as the physical landscape of Kezi and its environment, and after her death, the community confronts drought and the sickening and over-abundant smell of rot from the Marula tree. Thenjiwe is also clearly linked to the cave paintings of the stone virgins that Sibaso encounters in the Matopos thereby making this connection more obvious. This textual evidence confirms the representation of the older stone virgin in the earlier text and strengthens the argument that Thenjiwe represents Nehanda in Vera's latter novel.

Thus, the following lyrical description of the decapitation of Thenjiwe as she carries a bucket of water, a life giving force, on her head illustrates the desecration of the ancestral Nehanda mhondoro's legacy by the nationalist government:

> Thenjiwe...she calls. A man emerges. He is swift. Like an eagle gliding. His head is behind Thenjiwe, where Thenjiwe was before, floating in her body, he is in her body. He is floating like a flash of lightning. Thenjiwe's body remains upright while this man's head emerges behind hers, inside it, replacing each of her moments, taking her position in the azure of the sky. (Vera 66)

Thenjiwe, who can be closely linked with the Nehanda figure in *Nehanda* is suddenly without a head because an "eagle" has severed it. The soapstone fish-eagle recovered from the ruins of Great Zimbabwe graces the nation's flag and is a well-known nationalist symbol that cannot be overlooked in this passage. Furthermore, it is Sibaso's head that takes Thenjiwe's head's place above her body, but at this point in the narrative, he is still the unnamed soldier, an every-soldier. Thus, the Nehanda figure was traditionally revered as the ancestor spirit under whose leadership the people could unite; however, in this passage her figure is debased and she is no more than a puppet because her attacker is "in her body," impersonating her even after he has killed her.

Vera implies that Nehanda's leadership has been replaced by that of the nationalists who have cut away the true ancestral values and placed in their stead their own skewed focus on a one party state, which they want to control without opposition. The indigenous politicians and their military are destroying an ancestral icon and "replacing each of her moments, taking her position in the azure of the sky," and in the ancestral realm of the midzimu, with their own neo-colonial ideology. Sibaso's death dance with Thenjiwe is a clear illustration of one part of the betrayal trauma. Immediately after decapitating Thenjiwe, the violence turns toward Nonceba, who arguably represents the people of Zimbabwe. She is one of the sisters who is massacred in the indigenous village in Nehanda, but in The Stone Virgins she is left only half dead so that Vera can propose the notion of post-traumatic healing and deliverance for a nation that has been twice-traumatized.

As Nonceba stumbles upon the murder of her sister, she is so stunned that she cannot choose from the traditional western psychological paradigm of flight or fight. Thus, her attacker proceeds to hold her against her will, sexually assault her, and finally, remove her lips from her face so that she becomes wordless. While the younger sister is closely associated with the people, the crimes Sibaso commits against her mirror the kinds of state sponsored terror that was inflicted upon the civilian population. Sibaso holds her against her will and tries to "soothe her" while the government tries to soothe the people with nationalist rhetoric about safeguarding them against dissidents in an effort to hide that it also terrorized and "used emergency powers to enforce widespread curfews, roadblocks, detention without trial, and house to house searches" against the people of Matabeleland (CCJP 10). Sibaso also sexually assaults Nonceba, just as the governmental forces assault the civilians by killing them, beating them, and raping and sodomizing women. Finally, Sibaso cuts off Nonceba's lips with one swift movement, and in carrying out these violent actions against the civilian population and showing clear examples of what would happen to those who speak of the atrocities, such as public executions, torture, and rape, the nationalist government in effect silenced the people who suffered the most. Thus, the cutting away of Nonceba's lips clearly correlates with the violent silencing of the people as codified by the government in a series of actions and laws that insured silence until the CCJP's report in 1999.

As alarming as this set of betrayals is to the Zimbabwean people, Vera does not end the novel there because writing Nonceba's recovery allow her to tell a counter-narrative of potential rebirth and hope. While Nonceba's physical wounds heal slowly and her face is reconstructed so that "with some powder on, she looks almost unharmed. Almost." (153), she does carry on looking for "a type of rescue, a deliverance"(154). The acknowledgement of her suffering and that of her compatriots, envisioned in the concept of deliverance, would bring that psychic healing from betrayal trauma. Thus, she moves to Bulawayo, goes through reconstructive surgery which is "almost" successful, gets a job, and opens her heart to the possibility of hope that "a new nation needs to restore the past...deliverance" (165). Thus, Nonceba, as a representative of the

Zimbabwean people who is still silenced, looks to the future for hope, redemption, and words. In *Nehanda*, hope is foreshadowed by Vatete, Nehanda's aunt, who tells the title character "often we say that the mouth is like a wounded tree, it will heal itself" (24). Nonceba endures so that Zimbabwe will have a future and heal itself. She is not yet able to speak of the horrors she has witnessed, but she is a survivor and as such carries on until she can psychologically heal from the trauma and find, once again, "the certainty of her words" (161).

Thus, Yvonne Vera's two novels serve as testimonio to the traumatization of all the characters in her latter novel, for even the cultural tradition, which Vera defends and revives in her novel *Nehanda*, has become corrupt and complicit with colonialism and capitalism in the latter (Ranger 205). In *The Stone Virgins*, she gives voice to those betrayed by the horrors of the Matabeleland massacres and to the victimizers, who she reminds us, were created by repeated trauma and betrayal by the nationalist government, thereby experiencing a double traumatization that warped their humanity.

Chat

Chapter 8

Seven Nigerian Authors

G.M.T.Emezue

WHILE the editors of the International Council on African Literature and Culture might have busied with papers on the theme of Conflict and War in African literature for their current journal project, the organisers of the Nigerian Authors' (ANA) colloquium were doing a similar thing in Owerri, the headquarters of Imo state in Eastern Nigeria, the theme of their conference: "Literature and Conflict Resolution". Conflict, ever since world spotlight on African literature had engaged Achebe's *Things Fall Apart*, is proving a vexatious issue for many within and outside the criticism of literature in Africa and the New World.

The proceeding chat is of much significance to readers of African literature in that the objective of constant revaluation and reinventing of aesthetics and canons of African writing seems of profound critical relevance to our Conflict discussants. For these (seven) Nigerian writers and critics of African literature, namely, Odia Ofeimun, Elechi Amadi, Julianah Okoh, Chidi Maduka,

Femi Osofisan, JOJ Nwachukwu-Agbada, and the octogenarian poet, Gabriel Okara, who articulated various positions on the duty of the African writer today, there is no doubt that an African-centred perspective is at the heart of the argument on the Conflict question.

An interesting sidebar comes with Elechi Amadi's vaunted 'art for art's sake' argument. It is remarkable that while Amadi, who is Achebe's contemporary in the fictional re-inscription of the authentic African view of the universe, argues his favourite theory of writing for the sake of pure entertainment, others, in their diverse fashions, seem to lend credence to the ancient traditional position that literature must prove its relevance to social and environmental concerns of society.

Odia Ofeimun amplifies his distaste for non-ideological art, harping once more on his old disagreement with the elder J. P. Clark whose "practice of poetry" he confesses to have satirised in his poem "The Poet Lied" (168). Ironically Ofeimun, when he says the duty of literature is to 'purify language', sounds very much like Auden and McLeish whose ideas of 'literature that must be, and not mean' was dismissed offhand in his argument. Auden had talked about "defending one's language from corruption" as the only political duty of a poet. "When it is corrupted, people lose faith in what they hear" (qtd. in Achebe 35). Similarly Okara advises writers to be grounded on the language of narrative, even as Elechi Amadi emphasises reading as a prerequisite to good writing.

However, all seem to agree that the African writer must deepen not just his/ her vision (what Maduka has called "values") but also his/ her craft ("grounding in language" as per Gabriel Okara) in order to create literature that resolves individual and societal conflicts ("the writer's moral burden" ala Kole Omotoso) and endures in the hearts and minds of readers across many generations.

Not just be, but mean - ODIA OFEIMUN

The first duty of literature is to purify language so that the means of interaction between human beings will be at a level that does not debase meaning. One of the best ways to develop a language is to put it in a narrative mode. When it is narrative it means we can all share it even when we do not agree with what it is in the story. The truth is that a work of art in that sense is not like an essay, it is not a matter for debate. The truth that you will find in a story is supposed to remain forever no matter how circumstances change your language. Whereas, if you wrote an article you can come up with strong arguments another person can write another article with another set of strong arguments to demolish them. But with literature, every work of art has its own legitimacy and it is precisely because that is the case that you are able to have literature doing more than just presenting a problem. Literature does so many things at the same time because of its nature of not being just an argument. Therefore, when it resolves a conflict, it resolves a conflict by presenting you with a picture of reality that becomes a constant critique of what happens thereafter. There work of literature is always there. It does not change once you have written it down. And therefore, it serves as another reality that can critique whatever reality emerges. We (can only) assume, therefore that the values contained in that particular work of literature would be universal and perennial enough to continue serving as a critique. If it is good literature, that is what it is supposed to be... which is to say that if I hold a story about a situation of conflict, no matter how the story is resolved, it serves as a lesson to whoever else may come across it.

GMT Let me talk about the idea of literature serving a moral purpose. I remember that the American, Archibald McLeish, had stated that a poem should be and not mean...

OFEIMUN It should not just be, it should also mean. And the age in which all of them claimed that they were supporting a literature that is meant to be was one in which they thought they were moving away from a problematic ideology: the Marxist-Socialist ideology. Very many authors claimed that they were turning their back on that ideological position. In fact what they were doing was abandoning the human quotient in every situation. You find that many of the writers who adopted that line of action reversed themselves without having to apologize for it. When WH Auden wrote those lines, which our own J.P. Clark likes quoting a lot, that literature makes nothing happen; it is only a mouth..., the truth is that to have a mouth is already a basic critique of reality. There are those who have no mouth at all. Silence is not a critique of reality. But the fact that you have a mouth in itself means something. So that when a writer claims that poetry makes nothing change, it is like implying that it is wrong to be able to speak and we know that speaking has made it possible to have buildings, build cars and have all kinds of nice things in the world. It is therefore important to remember that those who are, those who can claim to be, are always obliged to speak; and to be able to speak at all is a very powerful weapon.

GMT Speaking especially for writers in the 21st century, are you then saying that literature should be a voice targeted mainly at social or political concerns...

OFEIMUN I'm actually offering a timeless position. I am saying that irrespective of when and where the literature is produced, it does the same things. That is you write a literature just to be, but because it is a demolition of silence, you have removed or put something in the environment. It is already providing you with a means of engaging the reality that you confront. Wherever literature is produced, it plays that role first of all, by just dealing with language. Language is a very important means of claiming humanity. Literature, to the extent that it consistently supports the idea of speech as a human quotient, supports our humanity. And so if we did not have speech, we would not be human. So you move it just a little. It is when you produce that you can say that this literature is one that is just be-ing. It also follows that what is in existence can fight. The fact that it exists at all means that somebody wedges a shoulder against that reality. Because literature will always do this, affect the language we use, and affect our perception of reality, it will always be a weapon of critique or a weapon of change. So that even the most conservative people in the world, producing a literature that is just supposed to be, end up offering what helps change the way the world looks like.

GMT Some say that is why in Africa most of the writings are still considered as mere protest literature. How do you respond to the criticism that the younger writers are merely upstarts in the field?

OFEIMUN You know when one generation passes judgment on another generation, we should always be very careful. Some young people dismiss older writers for one reason or another just like older writers dismiss younger ones. Usually that competition for space has no effect on literature because (usually) the critique of one set of production ends up becoming part of that. So no matter how they look at it, we belong to the same whirlpool. We are all being swept along by the same waves. So for me it is not a matter of debate whether the younger or older generation writer writes well or not.

Literature is for pleasure primarily - ELECHI AMADI

Writers are products of their society and in a society where you have turmoil and bickering over the national cake –bickering over injustice and so on– writers are bound to be sensitive over such things when they write about them. Nearly every book of poetry I pick up or which they give me is militant, decrying the injustice in the society at large. It is normal. The only danger there is that when you have too much commitment in your writing, the real literary quality may suffer. Well... and remember that literature is something meant to give pleasure to people. So if you concentrate too much on the vices in society and so on, you find the reader really gets bored and doesn't feel either elated or pleased. This is what I say and people say "Ah, you want to write escapist literature." It is not escapist literature. Literature is for pleasure primarily.

GMT Can you justify this position in light of current trends in the criticism of African literature which include the didactic or moral purpose of art. This criticism has included your own writings as well?

AMADI When you go to buy a book, a novel which you have not read before, what are you out for? You are out for entertainment. You are not out for facts on the Niger delta, or facts on oppression. You know that already. You are not out for the number of armed robbers in Imo State: you know that. Because these things are with you in the society. So when you pick up a novel, you are looking for something that is aesthetically pleasing. In a novel, there may be armed robbery, but the overall effect is to entertain you. So what I advice young writers is let's be committed to providing solution to society's many injuries but for goodness sake entertain your readers. That is why any person pays N200 (or) N500 to buy a book, they want to be entertained. They want to enjoy themselves. Within that entertainment you can now put in lots of militancy or whatever. But it shouldn't be the overall thing. There are some books of poems I read and from the first poem to the last, all is anger frustration, screaming at government and so on. Well the reader gets fed up and they wonder why the book is not popular. And the author wonders what went wrong: my grammar is correct etc. The only thing he hasn't done is that he has forgotten that his reader wants to be entertained.

GMT Writing for pleasure primarily, as you claim to practise, seems to have circumscribed the general reception of your works in Africa. Are you happy with the level of criticism your books have received so far?

GMT Oh yes, I am. I am not complaining. My works are global as you know. The other day somebody from Sri Lanka wrote to me. He said: I hope your government is paying you for advertising Nigerian culture all over the world. It is a global thing. We are no longer local. So whatever the critics here write, the global thing is becoming more and more important.

GMT How would you access the literature of our times vis-a-vis our older writings where your own works would rightly belong and the emerging tradition in Nigerian and African writing?

AMADI It tends to be militant, committed to social issues. It might have a little decline in quality but the output is quite prodigious and that is what matters. Since more people are writing, which hopefully means that more people are reading, quality comes with time and there is always the "good old days" syndrome. They think the good old days are better. Among the young ones writing, there are masterpieces which eventually will later be discovered. So I don't have any despair at all when it comes to the young ones writing. I remember two days a principal of one of the schools sent me a novel which kept me awake the whole night. I was really impressed. So I might say that while majority of the works are militant and heavily socially committed, there are some very good one amongst them.

GMT Some critics believe that the missing link is committed publishers. During your own time there were publishers who were out to discover and help the good writers. The scripts may have been good but then publishers helped, didn't they?

AMADI You are quite correct. There is need for committed publishers. People who are not too much after profit and who consider their publishing a societal service. When Heinemann started publishing, they didn't know they were going to make a success of it, but their keenness to project African literature was there and then they published. You know they prospered and sold well. Not all the books made it, but a few made it and they sold and covered up. But these days our publishers are very choosy. They want to make absolutely certain they recoup their money and so on. What we actually need is a consortium. A big consortium of publishers with big money who are willing to dare it and say: 'Ok we will publish. As long as the work has some merit we publish and see what happens.' Maybe if you publish a 1000 books, maybe 800 may not do so well. Or out of 100, 50 might not do very well and the other 50 will do very well. So you cover up your losses on the others. Though I agree that we need committed publishers but these publishers have to be made –like the big banks with heavy financial base. It's the same thing. We need a consortium of publishers with a heavy financial base who have no doubt about the feeling that not only are they out to make gains, but they are there to do social service as well. Writers don't have money. When we are talking about money for this kind of thing, we are talking about billions for instance.

GMT Then you do not find writing lucrative. Is that what Professor Amadi is telling us?

AMADI No, it is not lucrative enough to sustain anybody including myself. So I cannot depend on what they pay me. That is why I have to farm. I don't buy cassava, I don't buy vegetables. I live right in the village so I don't entertain heavily. Only very few friends come to the village so I live very simply.

GMT But you are still writing, we hope?

AMADI I have been writing. (There is) my book of essays *Speaking and Singing* and you haven't read my

176

latest play *The Woman of Calabar*? I'm still writing. The joy of writing and fortunately for me when I write people enjoy reading me. And if you write and give people pleasure, that is something to be happy about.

GMT Your readers hardly know you as a playwright, professor.

AMADI Well, I think they do. *Peppersoup* is very popular. Even *The Woman of Calabar*. So my plays are popular. The problem is that most people don't read. And we don't have theatre houses where every weekend you should be able to go see a play, relax and enjoy a good play. On weekends in a modern city like Port Harcourt we either go to a joint or night club. The play houses should be there to show a good play every weekend and that will now make for education of the public. But we don't have such a thing. Perhaps we need a consortium of dramatists who can now put up these plays and invite the public to come.

GMT How then would you imagine the future of Nigerian and African writing?

AMADI Many novelists and dramatists have had a field day. In fact they have a better opportunity than we had. In our days, you wouldn't dream of your books being made into a film or whatever. But nowadays, that is what is going on. The future is very, very bright for Nigerian literature.

GMT Maybe you can tell your readers something they often ask: what inspired you to write *The Concubine*?

AMADI I don't know. I believe it is just the creative instinct in me. I just found myself scribbling and it came out. And aided by the fact that I had read a lot. I was brought up in a very good school. I had read so many novels, the great works by Dickens, Hardy, Dumas etc. When you read through that kind of classic, you know you are living in the world of the novel. But the creative instinct has to be there before you can begin to write

Literature is first of all to educate - JULIA OKOH

Literature is not only to entertain. Literature is first of all to educate. Ok? They entertain, they educate. But if you are talking about literature for development or conflict resolution, while treating that subject the writer will like to show what is going on in the society because literature reflects society. And by reflecting society you bring out ideas about moral issues within. Thus conflict is resolved by showing the consequences of conflict. By talking about conflict, you also bring into moral issues like what is the purpose of this conflict? Is it helping our situation? Literature will help you to analyse these questions.

GMT Then you disagree with the claim for literature as pure entertainment project?

OKOH It was only at a particular time in history that the concept came out in Western writing. Right from the time of Greece, people had started to build on literature, developing their epics. It was not just entertainment. There were moral issues there. Literature even helped to revolutionize the world then. And if you are talking about the French revolution, literature helped to sensitise the people and let them know. It's like saying "see what is happening here, are we going to leave it like that?" Before the Russian revolution, the Russian people talked and wrote about their society and people got the idea to change them.

GMT Elechi Amadi has complained that African writing has become rather too committed...

OKOH Too committed? It can never be too committed. What I know is that we are still growing. We have not yet started appreciating literature further ahead than it is. Rather we are still at (the level of) political theatre; that is conscientizing the people; let(ting) people know what is going on and maybe show them the way forward. At least although we cannot give a medicine to cure, we can give ideas to cure. So that is African literature. By reading the meaning and asking: what is this author trying to say? we try to dig up solutions to our conflicts.

GMT Perhaps you also do not agree then that contemporary writers are too militant and therefore not so good?

OKOH Who said the works are not so good? Well, I haven't read all to know whether that is the situation, but many of the ones I have read are very good. The persons saying that they are not so good, what criteria are they using? I really don't understand the phrase "not so good." If you are not occupied with social issues, what else will they be writing about? What I will accept is that young writers are impatient and want to be known quickly. But the mature writer, they take their time to structure their work. Like Gabriel Okara said, you just don't jump up and start writing; you take time to read what has been written. The literary tools have been there for long. You have to dig them out and use them. But some of us, may be they want to be known immediately, so they don't work, they just get the story out. But others take their time. And to master it demands a lot of work. So you have to learn it. It is not inherited. You have to acquire it and that is what gives beauty to a good literary work. If you say from that perspective that most of them lack aesthetics, Ok. I can agree with that to some extent. But there are many authors here who are working on their work.

GMT What do you have to say generally or specifically about Nigerian and African writing?

OKOH Oh, we have a great future. But before long we are able to form a literary academy. I like what the French people did. Anything you write, there is French academy that regulates literature. We don't have any such academy in Nigeria. If we have it, then we will be able to make the best. In France, that academy regulates even words; the ones you can use and the ones you cannot use. But here we don't have such.

You don't entertain in a vacuum - CHIDI MADUKA

If you ask, literature basically deals with order, right? Literature as an art form uses words to champion the cause of order. So this order has been established and is being studied by other bodies, science, social sciences, education, etc. So they communicate explicitly, whereas for people in literature, literature communicates implicitly. Literature tries to harmonise other disciplines they cover. You see that all the time they centre on order; literature tries to emphasize order. Artistes, poets, playwrights they lay emphasis on order. They put words together to form certain patterns either chronologically or syntactically. They try to give a vision of life which may be political or not, but there has to be a vision. So the idea of literature and conflict resolution is appropriate although the formalist-oriented may think that it should be art for art's sake. In spite of that, any rich work tries to convey some element of values. And those elements of values may not even be political with the social and various levels of human existence. So for me, it (literature and conflict resolution) is appropriate.

GMT We have been accused of becoming too pre-occupied with social issues – a trend we had started since the sixties and brought into the 21st century...

MADUKA No, No, that is a false charge. As I said, there is no way a writer can evade what is happening around him even though among African writers (not even Europeans); there is a disagreement about what social role literature should do. If you remember, Elechi Amadi tells us that he is there as a novelist to entertain. But in fact he doesn't entertain in a vacuum. So that the essential thing about literature...is the necessity of championing the cause of other relationships between the individual and the society, and between the various actors on the drama of social change. You see in Africa, Africans have been persecuted, have been oppressed for centuries so that the political element, the political aspects of the struggle for order, dominates that experience. I said it somewhere when I was writing on Elechi Amadi that Elechi Amadi's *Estrangement* came before (Chinua Achebe's) *Anthills of the Savannah* but *Anthills of the Savannah* has more critical attention than *Estrangement* although *Estrangement* is a powerfully crafted novel, it is a very good novel. Why? Because of the importance of the dimension the author gives. That is what is prominent.

GMT Is it truly possible at this stage to distinguish the style of the older from the younger generation of African writers who are both walking in the same direction of resolution of the African conflict and other important issues of their times?

MADUKA African writers should simply study oral tradition. Many new writers no longer do this. They are rushing as if they are products of the CNN. But we have African culture. It has roots. So when colonialism came, we got English Language. English Language cannot capture the various essence of our cultural heritage. Our writers must learn to go back to the oral tradition. It is still important; more so since the values based on oral tradition are still very much with us.

GMT But the younger writers are not doing that. A young writer here was so brazen to say that he does not need oral literature. So they only write what Europeans and Americans want to read about Africa, and ironically they are lauded with awards which, to every extent, are misleading as far as our literary values remain in abject concealment. Since the west makes them feel they have arrived or that they are so good, there's hardly anything they can learn from tradition.

MADUKA Well, no, no. You know sometimes in writing there is uniqueness and greatness in every writer. It doesn't mean that we cannot get good works that are not rooted in oral tradition. But we have to call attention to every writer, whether you succeed without it, to go back to oral sources, to study our oral tradition very well. It doesn't mean that if one doesn't use it, one may not get an award. A writer is very sensitive to what people say: taxi drivers, market women, and when you come down to their level, you can capture some essence.

You can write what has populist appeal. But one can go further than that. I still recommend it (oral tradition). But it doesn't mean that one would be a failure if one doesn't use it. African society is very complex and it encompasses the traditional values. Even critics should remember this issue and not only writers.

We have many astute writers - FEMI OSOFISAN

There is nothing strange about the idea of literature and conflict resolution. Perhaps some people believe that literature is pure aesthetics, they just write for art's sake, but you also realise that in spite of this belief that it is otherwise: the writer as a member of the society has a duty to contribute to the society, as part of that society. He is able to contribute as a result of his own imagination, his intellectual prowess. The writer as a visionary is somebody who is able to offer perspectives. What better way to do this than with dealing with the problems of the society. The world is beset with so many conflicts. Yet we have to resolve them if we want to live together in such a way that literature responses to.

GMT But what role would aesthetics play for literatures that are merely preoccupied with conflicts and their resolutions?

OSOFISAN For it to be literature at all, it has to be aesthetically pleasing. Or it is not literature at all. That is, the first criterion is that it has to be readable, it has to be pleasing. So that is aesthetics for you. If it is literature, it has to have aesthetics; else it is not literature at all.

GMT This idea that our writers are overly preoccupied with social issues, so many of their works …

OSOFISAN Who are the writers that you are referring to?

GMT I refer to younger writers...

OSOFISAN But many of them are winning prizes. They are winning international prizes so how can you say that they are not writing well?

You can create a society where everything works - JOJ NWACHUKWU-AGBADA

In fact any writer who believes that his work has nothing to do with practical existence is like a hen on one leg. I believe literature can resolve conflict. I do not agree with Kole Omotoso (keynote speaker at the colloquium) that literature has nothing to resolve and also there is no win-win situation. That sounds rather prescriptive, because literature can also have a positive angle. We know that principally literature is always questioning; it is always asking why things are the way they are. But if there is a proposition and a writer takes it up to create a situation where there is a win-win situation, I don't see anything wrong with that except where, maybe, that's what the writer does all the time. But in a particular situation, if a writer chooses to do that, there is nothing wrong with it.

GMT Kole Omotoso had also talked about the moral burden; for a writer there must be a moral burden and they must not simply create situations that are resolved in a "win-win" situation. How do you see this proposal?

NWACHUKWU-AGBADA That "win-win" situation is also a moral burden. You can create a society where everything works. That's the idea of utopia. It can happen from time to time. But if somebody is utopian all the time, you can now accuse him of not understanding what literature is all about. Should we be writing tragedy all the time? No sometimes, it can be comic. Because if the word "comic" is not important, it would not have been in the dictionary of literature.

GMT Since we are talking about a "win-win" situation in art, what do think about the idea of writers attempting to create ideals within the traditional where ideal heroes exist and are celebrated. I know of a novel which has the characters existing in the ancestral planes where the people are ideal creations and always helping everyone to reconcile. ..

NWACHUKWU-AGBADA For sure, the "win-win" situation is most appropriate. Take the South African situation: The South Africa I know is the one presented in newspapers and other media. Well if you remember that there was a long, drawn-out struggle. ANC for instance was established in 1912, and from 1912 to 1994, you know how many years that is. The struggle was won when somebody realized within himself that there should be reconciliation. But if there is no reconciliation, what is left for us? How does society move? Are we saying that people can move on without being reconciled to each other? That's why I said that it is not a law that anybody writing should see it from a tragic situation. If we are in a situation where there is no resolution, ok? As we talk about ideals, a writer has ideals. Utopia is idealistic. So it can happen, or it cannot happen. After all the progress we have today in the sciences was born out of idealism: people going to space and what not. People wrote literature that others thought would never happen and it happened. We can project on reconciliation and there will be reconciliation. If we project on going to the moon, then we will go to the moon. But then in 1928 HG Wells talked about the first man in the moon and in 1957 it happened, so if we do that kind of thing, what's strange about it? It does happen.

GMT But then why do we prefer projecting the negative to affirming a positive condition nowadays? Is it not because the seamier the merrier, particularly if our books must appeal to the American market where we now crave recognition.

NWACHUKWU-AGBADA No, no it is not negative, because why writers do that is to shock us out of our complacency, ok. It is only by things sounding tragic that people's consciousness can be stirred. And I think some people's work will always remain tragic.

The writer might influence the thinking of people -
GABRIEL OKARA

Literature and Conflict resolution is an appropriate theme to deal on. You know there are many forms of conflicts. Conflicts that may end in violence and other non-violent conflicts and so on. But literature by exposing the society perhaps aims to bring peace and justice. Writers, you know, want justice to be done, however trivial and so on. There is a sense of justice in all of us. They support justice and by doing that the writer through his works might influence the thinking of the people. Through his writing and actions some changes will show, you know. (Thus) they resolve seemingly irreconcilable positions between two communities or two societies or within the society itself.

GMT So much has been said of tendencies among upcoming writers from this country. What is your view about the younger literatures? Are they overly preoccupied with social problems by your own assessment?

OKARA Their use of language is symptomatic of their grounding. Now in schools, as in universities, use of language is very poor. Even for graduates, I find many surprisingly inefficient in their knowledge of the language. And the situation of English in schools: primary schools, secondary schools and universities, shows how low the study and use of language (has become), how low the students acquire English Language over the years. At present it is the only medium through which the writer can best express themselves or tell their stories. (You also) find out that they are not literate in their own languages. So that's a problem that I think will resolve itself in future.

GMT At 80 years and over, are you working on anything at present?

OKARA I am working on two books. I don't want to give you the titles yet.

GMT Is there any chance they will come out this year?

OKARA Well, not this year (2007). I expected that one would come out this year but it couldn't. It will be next year (2008).

GMT When you were writing "Victoria Beach" what inspired you to it?

GMT Well, I don't know. (Smirks) Maybe you can tell me.

END

Notes and Bibliography

Chapter 1
Resisting Normative Definitions

Works Cited

Bessora. *Deux bébés et l'addition*. Paris: Serpent à Plumes, 2002.

− − −. "La question du genre: le cas feminine-masculin," Africultures 35, Jan. 1 (2002).

Bland, Lucy and Laura Doan. *Sexology Uncensored: The Documents of Sexual Science*. Chicago: University of Chicago Press, 1999.

Butler, Judith. *Gender Trouble: Feminism and the Subversion of Identity*. London: Routledge, 1999.

− − −. "Performative Acts and Gender Constitution: An Essay in Phenomenology and Feminist Theory." *Theatre Journal*, Vol. 40, No. 4 (Dec., 1988): 519-531.

− − −. *Undoing Gender*. London: Routledge, 2004.

Connell, R.W. Masculinities. Los Angeles: University of California Press, 1995.

De Meyer, Bernard. "La sage-femme, l'éxilée et l'écrivain ou les bébés hybrides de Bessora," *French Studies in Southern Africa*, No. 36 (2006): 16-30.

Dean, Carolyn. *The Frail Social Body: Pornography, Homosexuality, and Other Fantasies in Interwar France*. Berkeley: University of California Press, 2000.

Evans, David T. *Sexual Citizenship: The Material Construction of Sexualities*. London: Routledge, 1993.

McCaffrey, Edna. *The Gay Republic: Sexuality, Citizenship, and Subversion in France*. Burlington, VT: Ashgate Publishing Company, 2005.

Nagel, Joane. "Ethnicity and Sexuality," *Annual Review of Sociology*, vol. 26 (2002): 107-133.

− − −. "Masculinity and Nationalism: Gender and Sexuality in the Making of Nations." *Ethnic Racial Studies*. Vol. 21, no. 2, pp. 242-69.

Preciado, Beatriz. *Manifeste contra-sexuel*. Paris: Balland, 2000.

– – –. ÒMultitudes queer: notes pour une politique des anormaux,"
Multitudes, vol. 12, (2003): 17-25.

Schor, Naomi. "The Crisis of French Universalism," *Yale French Studies,
No. 100*, "France/USA: The Cultural Wars." (2001): 43-64.

Storr, Merl. "Postmodern Bisexuality," *Sexualities*, vol. 2/3 (1999).

Chapter 2
Gender Conflict in African Literature

Works Cited

Adebayo, Aduke. "Tearing the Veil of Invisibility: The Roles of West
African Female Writers in Contemporary Times". *Feminism &
Black Women's Creative Writing*. Ed. Aduke Adebayo, (Ibadan:
AMD Publishers) 1996 (37-56).

Barry, Peter. *Beginning Theory*. Manchester and New York:
Manchester University Press, 2002.

Bungaro, Monica. "Mothering Daughters and the Other Side of the
Story in Amma Darko, Ama Ata Aidoo and Nozipo Maraire"
*African Literature Today 25 (New Directions in African
Literature) Ed.* E. Emenyonu. New Jersey: Africa World Press,
2006 (76-81).

Cousins, Helen. "Submit or Kill Yourself…Your Two Choices
Options for Wives in African Women's Fiction" *New Women's
Writing in African Literature 24*. N.J.: African World Press. 2004
(104-114).

Emecheta, Buchi. *The Joys of Motherhood*. Ibadan: Heinemann, 2004.

Emenyonu, Ernest. (ed.) Goatskin Bags and Wisdom: *Critical
Perspective on African Literature*. Trenton: Africa World Press,
2000.

Fall, Aminata Sow. *The Beggars' Strike*. Ibadan: Spectrum, 2002.

Kolawole, M.E.M. "Womanism and African Consciousness." *African
Literature Today 24 (New Women's Writing in African Literature)*

Ed. E. Emenyonu. New Jersey: Africa World Press Inc., 2004 (104 - 114).

Ogot, Grace. *The Promised Land*. Nairobi: Heinemann, 1966.

Osammor, Stella Ify. *The Triumph of the Water Lily*. Ibadan: Kraftgriot, 1996.

Schipper, Mineke. "Buchi Emecheta" *Imagining Insiders: Africa and the Question of Belonging*. London: Cassell, 1999, (189-191).

Chapter 3
Gender and African Modernity

Notes
1.No Longer at Ease is abbreviated to [NLAE]
2.Anthills of the Savannah is abbreviated to [AS]

Works Cited

Achebe, Chinua. *No Longer at Ease*. London: Heinemann, 1967.

– – – . *Anthills of the Savannah*. New York: Anchor Press, 1988.

Carroll, David. *Chinua Achebe*. London: Macmillan, 1980.

Ekpa, Anthonia Akpabio. "Beyond Gender Warfare and Western Ideologies: African Feminism for the 21st Century." *Goatskin Bags and Wisdom: New Critical Perspectives on African Literature*. Ed. Ernest N. Emenyonu. Trenton, NJ: Africa World Press, 2000 (27-38).

Falola, Toyin. *Culture and Customs of Nigeria*. Westport: Greenwood, 2001.

hooks, bell. "Sisterhood: Political Solidarity between Women." *Dangerous Liaisons: Gender, Nation, and Postcolonial Perspectives*. Eds. Anne McClintock, Aamir Mufti and Ella Shohat. Minnesota: University of Minnesota Press, 1997. 396-411.

Hyden, Goran. *African Politics in Comparative Perspective*. Cambridge: Cambridge University Press, 2006.

Khayyoom, S.A. *Chinua Achebe: A Study of his Novels*. New Delhi: Prestige, 1999.

Mazrui, Ali A. "The Black Woman and the Problem of Gender: An African Perspective." *Race, Gender, and Culture Conflict: Debating the African Condition: Ali Mazrui and his Critics*. Eds. Mazrui Alamin M. and Willy M. Mutunga. Vol. 1. Trenton: Africa World Press, 2004 (212-235).

Njoku, Benedict Chiaka. *The Four Novels of Chinua Achebe: A Critical Study*. New York: Peter Lang, 1984.

Okeke, Philomena E. "Negotiating Social Independence: The Challenges of Career Pursuits for Igbo Women in Postcolonial Nigeria." *'Wicked' Women and the Reconfiguration of Gender in Africa*. Eds. Dorothy Hodgson L. and Sheryl A. McCurdy. Portsmouth, Heinemann, 2001 (234-251).

Palmer, Eustace. *An Introduction to the African Novel: A Critical Study of Twelve Books*. New York: Africana, 1972.

Reese, Lyn and Rick Clarke. *Two Voices from Nigeria: Nigeria through the Literature of Chinua Achebe and Buchi Emecheta*. California, Stanford Program on International and Cross-Cultural Education, 1985.

Chapter 4
Female Writers on War

Works Cited

Biko, Steve. *I Write What I Like*. London: The Browerdean P, 1978.

Boehmer, Elleke. *Colonial and Post-Colonial Literature*. Oxford: Oxford UP, 1995.

Brannigan, John. *New Historicism and Cultural Materialism*. New York: St. Martin's P, 1988 .

Brink, André. "Interrogating Silence: New Possibilities Faced by South African Literature." *Writing South Africa: Literature, Apartheid, and Democracy, 1970-1995*. Eds. Attridge Derek and Rosemary, Jolly. Cambridge: Cambridge U P, 1998. 14-28.

Cazenave, Odile. "Writing the Child, Youth, and Violence into the Francophone Novel from Sub-Saharan Africa: The Impact of Age and Gender." *Research in African Literatures 36.2. 2005.* 59-71.

Driver, Dorothy and Meg Samuelson, "History's Intimate Invasions: Yvonne Vera's The Stone Virgins." *The End of Unheard Narratives: Contemporary Perspectives on Southern African Narratives*. Ed. Bettina Weiss, Heidelberg: Kalliope Paperbacks, 2004. 175-208.

Edward N. *The Stanford Encyclopedia of Philosophy*. Stanford: Stanford U.2005 http://plato.stanford.edu/ entries/war December 2007.

Emecheta Buchi. *Destination Biafra*. Glasgow: Williams Collinsons, 1982.

Gagiano, Anne. "Entering the Oppressor's Mind: A Strategy of Writing in Bessie Head's A Question of Power, Yvonne Vera's *The Stone Virgins* and Unity Dow's *The Screaming of the Innocent*." *Journal of Commonwealth Literature. (2006); 41:* 43-60.

Gagiano Anne. "Reading The Stone Virgins as Vera's Study of the Katabolism of War." *Research in African Literatures 38.2. 2007.* 64-76.

Gordimer, Nadine. *None to Accompany Me*. New York: Penguin Books, 1994.

Gunner Liz et al. "Introduction: Yvonne Vera's Fictions and the Voice of the Possible." *Research in African Literatures 38.2 (2007)* 1-8.

Guerin L. Wilfred. *A Handbook of Critical Approaches to Literature*. Third Edition. New York: Oxford U P, 1982.

Howard , Jean. "The New Historicism in Renaissance Studies." *English Literary Renaissance 16, 1986*. 13-43.

Ibironke Olabode. "Chinua Achebe and the Political Imperative of the African Writer." *Journal of Commonwealth Literature. 36, 2001*.75-91.

Silko, Leslie Marmon. *Ceremony*. New York: Viking Penguins,1977.

Musila, Grace. "Embodying Experience and Agency in Yvonne Vera's Without a Name and Butterfly Burning" *Research in African Literatures 38.2 Bloomington: Indiana U P (2007)* 49-63.

"Nigerian Civil War." *Wikipedia, the free Encyclopedia*. 2nd January 2008 http://en.wikipedia.org/wiki/Biafran_War. January 2008.

Ngugi wa Thiong'o. *Homecoming: Essays on African and Caribbean Literature, Culture and Politics*. New York: L. Hill, 1973.

Okuyade Ogaga. "The Rhetoric of Despair in Chin Ce's Children of Koloko." *Journal of African Literature and Culture*. IRCALC 2007 169-186.

O'Rielly, Christopher. *Post-Colonial Literature*. London: Cambridge UP, 2001.

"PSTD". *Review*. 9/11/2006. http://www.medicinenet.com/posttraumatic_stress_disorder/index.htm

Said, Edward W. *Representations of the Intellectual*. New York: Vintage Books, 1994.

Samuelson, Meg. "Yvonne Vera's Bulawayo: Modernity, (Im)mobility, Music, and Memory." *Research in African Literatures 38.2* Bloomington: Indiana U P. 2007. 22-35.

"War." Encyclopedia Britannica, 2006. eNotes.com. 2006. 7 Jan, 2008 <http://www.enotes.com/britannica-encyclopedia/

Vera, Yvonne. *The Stone Virgins*, Harare: Weaver Press, 2002.

Zaleza Paul. "Colonial Fictions: Memory and History in Yvonne Vera's Imagination." *Research in African Literatures 38.2 Bloomington: Indiana U P, 2007.* 9-21.

Chapter 5
Male Authority, Female Alterity

Works Cited

Amadiume, Ifi. *Male Daughters, Female Husbands: Gender and Sex in an African Society.* London: Zed Books, 1986.

Amuta, Chidi. *Towards a Sociology of African Literature.* Oguta: Zim Pan-African Publishers, 1986.

– – –. *The Theory of African Literature.* London: Zed Books Limited, 1989.

Carter, Cynthia et al eds. *News, Gender and Power.* London and New York: Routledge, 1998.

Chukukere, Gloria. *Gender Voices and Choices: Redefining Women in Contemporary African Fiction.* Enugu: Fourth Dimension Publishers, 1995.

Daly, Mary. *Beyond God the Father: Toward a Philosophy of Women's Liberation.* Boston: Beacon Press, 1977.

Hay, Jean and S. Stitchter, eds. *African Women South of the Sahara.* New York: Longman Limited, 1995.

Jacobus, Mary. *First Things: The Maternal Imaginary in Literature, Art and Psychoanalysis.* New York and London, 1995.

Julien, Eileen. *African Novels and the Question of Orality.* Bloomington, Indianapolis: Indiana University Press, 1992.

Kenyatta, Jomo. *Facing Mount Kenya.* London: Secker and Wamburg, 1938.

Kosky, Jeffrey. "Alterity." *Encyclopedia of Postmodernism.* Eds. Victor E. Taylor and Charles E. Winquist. London and New York: Routledge, 2001.

Mazrui, Ali. *The African Renaissance: A Triple Legacy of Skills, Values and Gender.* Lagos: CBAAC, 2000.

O' Barr, J. and Firmin-Sellers, "African Women in Politics." *African Women South of the Sahara*. Eds. Jean Hay and Stichter. New York: Longman, 1995 (189-195).

Osofisan, Femi. *Literature and the Pressures of Press Freedom*. Ibadan: Opon Ifa, 2002.

Pratt, Mary Louise. *Imperial Eyes: Travel Writing and Transculturation*. London: Routledge, 1992.

Spivak, Gayatri C. "Can the Subaltern Speak?" *The Post- Colonial Studies Reader* Eds. Bill Ashcroft et al. London and New York: Routledge, 1995 (24-28).

Stratton, Florence. *Contemporary African Literature and the Politics of Gender*. London: Routledge, 1994.

Taylor, J. Patrick. "Authority." *The Encyclopedia of Postmodernism*. Eds. Victor E. Taylor and Charles E. Winqiust. London and New York: Routledge, 2001.

Tsaaior, James Tar. "Gender Politics in Tiv Oral Narratives". PhD Thesis, Department of English, University of Ibadan, 2005.

Young, Crawford. *The Politics of Cultural Pluralism*. Ibadan: Heinemann, 1993.

Chapter 6
Feminist (Re-) Writing

Works Cited

Benstock, Shari, ed. *Feminist Issues in Literary Scholarship*. Bloomington & Indianapoli: Indian University Press, 1987.

Brown, Llyod W. *Women Writers in Black Africa*. Westport, CT: Greenwood Press, 1981.

Cabral, Amilca. "The Role of Culture." *Postcolonialism: An Historical Introduction*. Ed. Robert J. C Young. Oxford: Oxford University Press, 2001. 288-292.

Cartwright, John. *Political Leadership in Africa*. London and Canberra: Croom Helm, 1983.

Egudu, R. N. *Modern African Poetry and the African Predicament*. London and Basingstoke: MacMillan Press, 1978.

Ellis, Sarah. *The Women of England, the Social Duties, and Domestic Habits.* New York: D. Appleton and Co. 1839. *Feminsit Issues in Literary Scholarship.* Ed. Shari Benstock. Bloomington/Indianapolis: Indiana University Press, 1987.

Emecheta, Buchi. *Destination Biafra.* Oxford: Heinemann, 1994.

Friedman, Susan Standford. "Women's Autobipgraphical Selves: The Theory and the Practice." *The Private Self:Theory and Practice of Women's Autobiographical Writings.* Ed. Shari Benstock. London: Routledge, 1988. 34-62.

Hemingway, Ernest. *The Old Man and the Sea.* New York: Charles Scribner's Sons, 1952.

Jayawardena, Kuumari. *Feminism and Nationalism in the Third World.* London: Zed Books, 1986. In Postcolonalism: An Historical Introduction. Robert J.C. Young. Oxford: Blackwell Publishers Ltd., 2001: 360-78.

Keller, Edmond J. "Decolonization and the Failure of Politics." *Africa. 3rd ed.* Eds. Phillis M. Martin and Patrick O'Meara. Bloomington, Indiana: Indiana Univresity Press,1995. 164-71.

Knox, Bernard M.W. and William G. Thalmann. "Ancient Greece and the Formation of the Western Mind." *Norton Anthology to World Literature. 2nd ed; Vol 1.* Ed. Sarah Lawall. New York & London: W.W. Norton & Co., 2002. 104 - 803.

Markovitz, Irving Leonard. *Power and Class in Africa: An Introduction to Change and Conflict in African Politics.* Englewood Cliffs, NJ: Prentice-Hall, Inc., 1977.

Mbarga, Prince Nico. "Sweet Mother." Tilda and Rocafill Jazz International. Onitsha, Nigeria: Roger all Stars Nigeria Limited, 2007.

Mwaria, Cheryl B. Silvia Federici, and Joesph McLaren, eds. *African Visions: Literary Images, Political Change, and Social Struggle in Contemporary Africa.* Westport, Connecticut: Greenwood Press, 2000.

Newton, Judith. "Making - and Remaking - History: Another Look at Patriarchy." *Feminist Issues in Literary Scholarship.* Ed. Shari Benstock. Bloomington/Indianapolis: Indiana University Press, 1987. 124- 141.

Ng, Su Fang. "Women's Utopic Impulses in Buchi Emecheta's Destination Biafra." *Postcolonial Perspectives on Women Writers from Africa, the Caribbean, and the U.S.* Ed. Martin Japtok. Trenton, NJ: African World Press, 2003.

Obafemi, Olu. "Towards Feminist Aesthetics in Nigerian Drama." *Critical Theory and African Literature Today. 19*. Eds. Eldred D. Jones, Eustace Palmer, & Marjorie Jones. Trenton, NJ: African World Press, 1994: 84-100.

Porter, Abioseh M.. "They Were There, Too: Women and the Civil War(s) in Destination Biafra." *Emerging Perspectives on Buchi Emecheta*. Ed. Marie Umeh. Trenton, NJ: African World Press, 1992. 313 32.

Shakespeare, Williams. *Macbeth. The Riverside Shakespeare: Complete Works*. 2nd ed. Eds. G. Blakemore Evans and J.J. M. Tobin. Boston: Houghton Mifflin Co., 1997. 1360-1387.

Sudarkasa, Niara."The Status of Women in Indigenious African Societies." *Women in Africa and the African Diaspora*. Eds. Rosalyn Terborg-Penn et al. Washington, D.C: Howard University Press, 1987.25-43.

Spiro, Herbert J: *Politics in African: Prospects South of the Sahara*. Englewood Cliffs, N.J.: Prentice-Hall, 1964.

Stratton, Florence. *Contemporary African Literature and the Politics of Gender*. London and New York: Routledge, 1994.

Tomm, Winnie. "Ethics and Self-knowing: The Satisfaction of Desire." *Explorations in Feminist Ethics: Theory and Practice*. Eds. Eve B. Cole and Susan Coultrap-McQuin. Bloomington and Indianapolis: Indiana University Press, 1992. 102-110.

Uwakweh, Pauline A. "Female Choices: The Miliitant Option in Buchi Emecheta's Destination Biafra and Alice Walker's Meridian." *Nwanyibu: Womanbeing and African Literature. No. 1. 47 -60*. Eds. Phanuel A. Egejuru and Ketu H. Katrak.Trenton, NJ: African World Press, 1997. 47-61.

Young, Robert J. C. *Postcolonialism: An Historical Introduction*. Oxford: Oxford University Press, 2001. 274-92.

Chapter 7
Twice-Betrayed People

Notes

1.Yvonne Vera has called for "opening new spaces" for African literature by indigenous women and for women's counter-narratives in a literary setting that has so often silenced them or allowed them to be heard only through men's narratives. Thus, she named her edited collection of African women's writing *Opening Spaces: An Anthology of Contemporary African Women's Writing*. London: Heinemann, 1999.

2.See the following Caruth books for an overview of her development of and work with Trauma Theory: Trauma: Explorations in Memory (1995); Unclaimed Experience: Trauma, Narrative, and History (1996).

3.See David Healy's Images of Trauma for an analysis of hysteria and its connections to Freud and Janet's work on the subject.

4.Vera said of the creation of the Nehanda legend: "That's where I see a concentration of all our beliefs and what makes up our identity as a people, how we create legends and even how we recreate our history (Bryce 221). Similarly, Nana Wilson-Tagoe argues that Vera's 1993 novel contests history and the way it is disseminated so that Nehanda's legend points to a future constrained with less traditional history and more open to freeing spaces in both the realms of the secular and the spiritual (164).

5.For the historical counterpart to Yvonne Vera's treatment of Nehanda and the Matopos, see T. O. Ranger's Voices from the Rocks: Nature, Culture, History in the Matopos Hills of Zimbabwe. Harare: Baobab, 1999.

6.These mass assaults on indigenous civilians and former combatants were perpetrated in the interest of creating a one-party political state (ZANU) although the undeclared conflict was couched in more soothing terms of suppressing armed dissidents (read ZAPU) who were creating chaos across the country.

7.In 1982, the government intensified its assault on the civilian population by unleashing the Fifth Brigade, whose Shona name was "Gukurahundi" or the rain that washes away the chaff before the spring rains (CCJP 11), a Korean trained army unit answerable only to the Prime Minister, thereby eliminating any accountability for its collective actions in Matabeleland North where it was to operate.

8.Terence Ranger, prominent historian of Zimbabwe and close friend of Vera, noted similarly that after "having read Vera no one can ever again say that in comparison with other African slaughters 'not too many people' were killed in Matabeleland in the 1980s; no one can ever again fail to understand how important it still is to rescue the dead of Kezi from "vultures and unknown graves" and to reintegrate them into the society of the living" (212).

Works Cited

Bulhan, Hussein Abdilahi. *Frantz Fanon and the Psychology of Oppression.* New York: Plenum Press, 1985.

Bloom, Sandra. "Trauma Theory Abbreviated" *Final Action Plan: A Coordinated Community-Based Response to Family Violence.* Attorney General of Pennsylvania's Family Violence Task Force, October 1999.

Bryce, Jane. "Interview with Yvonne Vera, 1 August 2000, Bulawayo, Zimbabwe: 'Survival Is in the Mouth.'" *Sign and Taboo: Perspectives on the Poetic Fiction of Yvonne Vera.* Ed. Robert Muponde and Mandivavarira Maodzwa-Taruvinga. Harare: Weaver, 2003. 217-227.

Caruth, Cathy. "Unclaimed Experience:" *Trauma, Narrative, and History.* Baltimore: Johns Hopkins, 1996.

Catholic Commission for Justice and Peace (CCJP) and Legal Resources Foundation. Breaking the Silence: Building True Peace: A Report on the Disturbances in Matabeleland and the Midlands, 1980 to 1988. Harare: CCJP and LRF, 1997.

Fanon, Frantz. *The Wretched of the Earth.* London: Pluto, 1963.

– – –. *Black Skins, White Masks.* New York: Grove, 1968.

Flame. Dir. Ingrid Sinclair. Perf. Marian Kunonga and Ulla Mahaka. California Newsreel,1996.

Freyd, J. J. (2005) What is Betrayal Trauma? What is Betrayal Trauma Theory? 10 Dec. 2005 <http://dynamic.uoregon.edu/~jjf/defineBT.html>.

Gaidzanwa, Rudo. *Images of Women in Zimbabwean Literature.* Harare: College Press, 1985.

Herman, J.L. *Trauma and Recovery: The Aftermath of Violence -from Domestic Abuse to Political Terror.* New York: Basic Books, 1992.

– – –. "The Case of Trauma and Recovery: Conversations with Judith Herman, MD." Conversations with History. Institute of Intern! ational Studies. UC Berkley. 10 Dec. 10, 2005 <http://globetrotter.berkeley.edu/people/Herman/herman-con3.html>.

Lan, David. *Guns and Rain: Guerrillas and Spirit Mediums in Zimbabwe.* Berkeley: U of California Press, 1985.

Ranger, Terence. "History Has Its Ceiling: The Pressures of the Past in The StoneVirgins". *Sign and Taboo: Perspectives on the Poetic Fiction of Yvonne Vera.* Ed. Robert Muponde and Mandivavarira Maodzwa-Taruvinga. Harare: Weaver, 2003.203-216.

Vera, Yvonne. *Nehanda.* Harare: Baobab, 1993.

– – –. *The Stone Virgins*. Harare: Weaver, 2002.

Wilson-Tagoe, Nana. "Narrative, History, Novel: Intertextuality in the Historical Novels of Ayi Kweit Armah and Yvonne Vera." *Journal of African Cultural Studies 12.2 (1999)*: 155-166.

Chapter 8
Seven Nigerian Authors

Works Cited

Auden, W. H. Interview. *Morning Yet on Creation Day*. Chinua Achebe. Nairobi: Heinemann 1970

Ofeimun, Odia. *The Poet Lied*. Lagos: Update Communications, 1989.

Oral Traditions

WHILE much has been studied by literary scholars of the oral repertoire, and its significance for modern writing, attempts to maintain a uni-dimensional study of oral craft have not yielded the desired coherent and contemporaneous application of orality to literature. Ironically, the study of oral literature as a genre existing on its own terms and structures and formulae has only tended to place the traditions in pristine isolation from contemporary literary developments. Regrettably, oral studies (orature) have waned on the syllabi of many African universities as the written form seems to eclipse the oral space.

Our commitment to the study in oral traditions is borne from the awareness that African verbal arts still survive in works of discerning writers, and in the conscious exploration of its tropes, perspectives, philosophy and consciousness, its complementary realism, and ontology, for the delineation of authentic African response to memory, history and all possible confrontations with modern existence such as witnessed in recent analyses of the African novel. These studies use multi-faceted theories of orality which discuss and deconstruct notions of history, truth-claim, identity-making, genealogy (cultural and biological), and gendered ideologies.

Our Critical Approaches

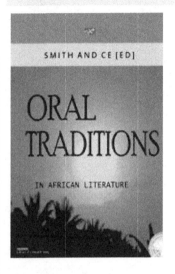

SMITH AND CE [ED]

ORAL TRADITIONS

IN AFRICAN LITERATURE

Liberian professor of African languages and literature, founder of the Society of African Folklore, and Literary Society International, LSi, Charles Smith, is editor of the Critical Writing Series on African Literature with Nigerian Chin Ce, books, news, reviews editor and research and creative writer. As one of the younger stream of poets from Africa, Ce is also the author of several works of fiction and essays on African and Caribbean literature.

Our Mission

African Books Network

AFRICAN Books Network with its cosmopolitan outlook is poised to meet the book needs of African generations in times to come.

Since the year 2000 when we joined the information highway of online solutions in publishing and distribution, our African alliance to global information development excels in spite of challenges in the region. Our select projects have given boost to the renaissance of a whole generation of dynamic literature. In our wake is the harvest of titles that have become important referrals in contemporary literary studies. With print issues followed by eContent and eBook versions, our network has demonstrated its commitment to the vision of a continent bound to a common world heritage. This universal publishing outlook is further evidenced by our participation in African Literature Research projects. For everyone on deck, a hands-on interactive is the deal which continues to translate to more flexibility in line with global trends ensuring that African writers are part of the information revolution of the present times.

As one of Africa's mainstream book publishing and distribution networks, writers may look forward to privileged assistance regarding affiliate international and local publishing and distribution service

"Our select projects at African Books Network have given boost to the renaissance of a whole generation of dynamic literature."